Retirement is a Blast!

Once You Light the Fuse

To Marty,
Light the
Fuse —

Terry Cummins

Terry
Cummins

ISBN: 1456338161
ISBN-13: 9781456338169

There is a candle in your heart, ready to be kindled. There is a void in your soul, ready to be filled. You feel it, don't you?

-Rumi

Contents

❉ ❉ ❉

CHAPTER I

I'M STILL UP THERE

❊ ❊ ❊

On my 64th birthday, some of my friends intended to bring a candle for the celebration, but they forgot to pack it. It would have been difficult lighting a candle on a 17,500-foot summit, because fire requires oxygen. Later that evening at dinner, they presented me with a modified birthday cake molded out of chocolate bars. It had one lit candle on top, the one they had forgotten to take to the summit.

The celebration was in a crowded tent near the base of Pyramide Blanca in the Andes Mountains in Bolivia, South America. On that memorable birthday, I had made my first technical climb to a summit using ropes, crampons, ice axes and all the other necessary gear, which seemed to weigh more than I did.

The candle remains on my desk as a reminder that all it takes to blast off is to stick your neck out the window of a retirement rocket ship and light the fuse. To celebrate life no matter the age requires a determined will, considerable effort and confidence that taking a risk will result in a successful touchdown. Soon after completing one adventure, you crawl into another rocket ship and blast off again.

Months later, I was asked if, after reaching the summit, and descending left a diminished or empty feeling. My response was, "No, I'm still up there." I will never come down from that high. That is what retirement should be—getting on a high and remaining there.

Our lives are divided into three phases—preparing to do something, doing it, and then not doing much of anything during the retirement or so-called golden years. I had a weird uncle, who skipped the second phase and semi-retired at the age of 21. You know the kind. Actually, we lead two lives, or two distinct phases of a continuous one. During the first sixty years, or thereabouts, we essentially do what we are told to fulfill the expectations necessary to make a living and, in most cases, raise a family. The journey is long, often arduous, and a continuous series of meeting one demand, requirement and responsibility after another. If all goes reasonably well, we overcome the burdens encountered, whether they were temporary or enduring, great or small.

Your first life began when the doctor spanked your butt and you wept and wailed at the shocking introduction. The second life begins when the boss kisses your butt goodbye on retirement day. You will weep that day, too, but not because of sadness. You will weep tears of joy, because unlike your first life, you begin to call the shots during your second one.

Neither of my two lives has been extraordinary like those noted individuals who performed great deeds and made lasting contributions. However, all lives are extraordinary in the sense that life is adventurous with its risks, dangers and the unknown. I do not consider my life remarkable as such, but perhaps, as Robert Frost noted, I am taking "a road less traveled by" during my second life that is making all the difference.

My first life was an adventurous one. I grew up on a hill farm in Kentucky, plowed tobacco and corn with horses, read by kerosene lamp and attended a four-room school. After graduating from college and then serving two years in the U.S. Navy, I raised a family and worked my front and backside off. Four children including twins in a little over four years with one wife is a continuing adventure like no other. In addition, spending 33 years in public schools, primarily as a high school principal and administrator, was like being in a flimsy lifeboat on a turbulent sea and never spotting land. It was 33 years of if-you-ain't-seen-it-yet-you-will kind of experience. Most of the associations with the kids and teachers were interesting, exciting and a few were heartbreaking. My duty was to simply contain a 2,7000 kids, 150 teachers, janitors, cooks and clerks in a building each day and keep them happy while maintaining the peace. It was extremely demanding maintaining the peace, so I prayed. "Please Lord, grant me some peace."

After nearly 60 years when the elbows ran low on grease and the "near empty" warning light came on, I said take this job and offer it to a younger person. However, I have few regrets about the rewarding course my first life took. I had not completely planned the second phase, but the official retirement day abruptly presented opportunities to do some of the things I had waited for years to do. Not only would there be ample time for leisure activities—golf, fishing, travel and various puttering-around-the house-time-wasters—but opportunities for more constructive endeavors. If the calendar-filled leisure pursuits became a drag, I could always get a job of some sort, start a small business, sell insurance or real estate (don't think so), volunteer for a worthy cause or perhaps join the Peace Corps.

Having grown up on a farm, I had always intended to return to nature and live off the land, raising and preserving natural foods from my orchards and vegetable gardens. I could even get a cow for milking and make butter and cheese. The one hindrance to having a cow is that the tank requires draining twice a day, which interferes with mountain climbing.

In addition to the desire to return to the land, writing was another endeavor I intensely wanted to pursue. I was a mediocre English major in college, but the works of the great authors fascinated me. How did those guys put words together like that? Occasionally, a thought or description, sentence or paragraph in one of my themes or term papers would be marked in red as "very good." The numerous other red marks indicated I should perhaps consider concentrating on physical education where it is body over mind. The problem I had was difficulty coming up with something to write about and then putting it into a series of words above an eighth-grade literacy level. The one time I approached literary renown was writing a critical essay on the great Greek dramatist, Euripides. The prof's statement on the title page marked in brilliant red slapped me squarely in the academic ego. "It's spelled E-u-r-i-p-i-d-e-s (stupid), not E-u-r-i-p-e-d-e-s." To this day, I get i and e confused.

The interim years of demanding and undivided attention to family and profession left little time to write. However, if Robert Frost could write about mending walls and stopping by a woods, why couldn't I? Emily Dickinson wrote, "I'm Nobody-Who are You? Are You-Nobody-Too?" I've had similar thoughts. Although I had dabbled a bit with the written word for 40 years, someday I thought I'd sit before a blank piece of paper, and as one author said, "open a vein."

In 1968, twenty-three years before retirement, unexpectedly, I was offered an opportunity to take my first trip abroad. Little did I realize it would be the first of 15 trips to other places in the world.

Being a high school principal at the time, I was selected by the National Association of Student Councils along with 27 other principals, counselors, teachers and nurses to assist sponsoring 133 high school juniors on an eight-week European Tour for

World Understanding. The logistics of organizing such an endeavor was similar to planning the D-Day invasion, and our primary goal was to keep casualties to a minimum.

The 160 Americans gathered in Washington D. C. for a couple days orientation. You can try to orient 133 16-year-old kids, but they already know it all. They were great, though, and all went well until we arrived at Dulles Airport for an 8 o'clock departure, which was delayed for nine hours. The word was that in preparing the plane for London, the sewage technician pushed the "blow" button rather than the "suction" button when cleaning the tiny toilets.

After finally landing in London and touring Europe, not only did I gain a better understanding of a new and different world, I learned that kids can be worn down to the point where they'll sleep on concrete. I also learned that, in most respects, the young have similar characteristics, goals and desires despite cultural and language differences. They rapidly form close ties and friendships, willingly give and share. The young people living on the European continent shared an important part of their 60's culture, which our kids readily adopted—shockingly, Beatle hairstyles and mini-skirts.

During the early part of the tour, some of our group attended services at Westminster Abbey in London. The abbey is quite different from the Short Creek Baptist Church in Kentucky, where I was either saved, or thought I was. Our church was smaller than the foyer of Westminster Abbey and we never had anyone important like a queen to visit us. In the cold wintertime, we huddled around a big heating stove in the center of the church to stay thawed. In hot summers, we used funeral-home fans to fight off wasps, which apparently preferred building their nests in a house of God. When the preacher heated up, you would hear a "whack." One time Orvil whacked Daisy's head when a wasp landed on her bonnet. The only similarity of the two churches was that both relied on the King James Version of the Bible.

There I was sitting in Poet's Corner over the burial sites of Chaucer, Shakespeare, Dickens and many other literary greats. It was surreal until the minister gave a plain, simple and inspiring sermon. His used the text from John 21:15-17. Upon leaving the service, I had the title for the book I had to write. Thirty-four years later, I wrote *Feed My Sheep,* a memoir about my growing up on the farm with my grandfather, whose character and goodness met the "good shepherd" standard. He lived his life feeding his sheep.

That first journey planted a seed. Someday, I would take other trips. As Yogi Berra, who played baseball on diamonds while expressing gems of wisdom about life, advised, "When you come to a fork in the road, take it." Choosing a fork on a less traveled road presents a dilemma. At the time of retirement, the age and fatigue factors usually prompt us to travel a safe and secure road. Why veer off an easy road to an uncertain fork where there are signs posted indicating "use caution," "dead end" or "no exit"? It is easier to continue rushing over crowded four-lane expressways and make a few rounds walking through a mall to keep the body in shape, with little regard for what it does to one's mind.

Most years when my four children were young, we managed to squeeze in a few brief vacations. When my children had nearly finished school, the cost of which would have financed passage on a moon mission, I decided to take a different type vacation. I had sacrificed my body and nervous system in completing the compulsory zoo visits, endless little league games and recitals for beginners. To complete a father's responsibility, I took my kids on the Mecca-like pilgrimage to Disney World. Shortly after my children reached puberty, it seemed like they began having children This necessitated a new responsibility in meeting the high standards set forth in the books about how to be a loving and caring grandfather. "Dad, don't you want to teach little Timmy how to fish?"

"No, I don't. Age and experience has taught me that sharp fish hooks are too dangerous."

With more time during summers and wanting to get away and do something different, I volunteered for an Earthwatch project in Peru. Earthwatch Institute is a non-profit organization engaging people worldwide in scientific field research to promote the understanding and action necessary for a sustainable environment. The organization provides excellent opportunities for retirees and others to contribute to environmental and scientific research. Under the direction of archeologists, anthropologists, veterinarians, doctors and other scientists, volunteers work on projects at the sites. The costs are reasonable and include meals and lodging, which is often in tents, and most of the volunteer expenses are tax deductible. An anthropologist and a professor of ancient architecture directed our project in Peru. The architect had previously conducted research on how the Incas mined the huge stones and constructed such incredible structures. Our project involved studying, measuring and surveying Chacha Bomba, an Inca ruin located on the banks of the Urubamba River flowing through the valley beneath the renowned Lost City, Machu Picchu. Although the exact purpose of why Chacha Bomba was constructed is unknown. One assumption is that with its numerous small rooms or compartments, which were possibly baths, it was a type of ceremonial site.

To get there, I flew to Lima, Peru, and then to Cuzco, a small, quaint city high up in the Andes. Its airport is one of the highest in the world at over 11,000 feet. Step off the plane and the sudden lack of oxygen affects your lungs as a week-long food fast would affect your stomach. After a slow saunter to the terminal, I sat for a while to acclimatize. To assist the process, the locals provide cups of coco tea. Yep, it is from the same leaves ground into white powder and sniffed up the nostrils. Coco tea contains 14 complex alkaloids and reputedly lowers the heart rate during drastic changes in altitude. Whether the tea lowered or raised my heart rate, I do not know, but my heart underwent a definitive change during my first exotic adventure.

From Cuzco, we traveled by land rover approximately 60 miles over rough winding roads to the project site. All during the ride, a very low cloud cover shielded the mountains from my view. The next morning, I awoke to a brilliantly clear day under a canopy of majestic snow-capped peaks. I have walked, run and plowed the hills of our Kentucky farm and gazed in awe at the Rockies and the Alps, but the Andes, the second highest mountain range in the world, were higher than I had ever imagined.

A certain mystique and power emanates from the higher peaks. The effect can be rather overpowering, as a sense of serene peace glides softly down from where clouds of blowing snow vaporize in the purest distant air. It's like a combination of massive bolts of energy thrust down, but with a mystically soothing and calming effect that tranquilizes. It's as if some sort of celestial being is inviting you to rise to its lofty abode. After the first observation, I kept looking up with one persistent thought, "How in God's name do they ever climb to the top of those things?" Eleven years later, I learned.

After completing the two-week project at Chacha Bomba, our team went to nearby Machu Picchu, where we camped and wandered around the famed ruins for a couple days. The mystery as to why and for what purpose Machu Picchu was constructed has never been completely resolved. Was it a retreat for the rulers of the largest empire in the world at that time, or was it a citadel, religious shrine, or sacred site? How did the Incas quarry the huge boulders, some weighing up to 15 tons, and transport them considerable distances up and down mountainsides to build such sturdy and lasting structures? During the past seven centuries in that area, earthquakes have leveled many other man-made structures, but much of what the Incas built has withstood the ravages of time. How they moved such giant boulders up the sides of mountains defies logic. You have to see the craftsmanship and the intricate patterns of perfectly carved stones to believe it. The massive stones fit perfectly when placed on top of another. Seven centuries later, architects and engineers struggle to keep roofs from leaking.

After setting up camp in the valley, we walked up the steep, rocky path to the fabled Lost City. Joan, a team member and pediatrician from Boston, and I decided to climb the towering granite peak, Huayna Picchu. It is adjacent to and overlooking the famed ruin. Most photographs show the peak as if it were a guardian, protecting the sacred shrine. After more than an hour climbing a very steep path carved out by the Incas centuries ago, we reached the Moon Temple at the top. Four years after my first incredible view from that high peak, I retired, in part, to have opportunities to climb up to other types of "moon temples." Truly, from those elevated vantage points, one can view a much wider expanse of this amazingly beautiful world.

In late afternoon, the groups of tourists departed on the four-hour train ride back to Cuzco. Alone, I wandered through the mystical ruin. As the sun began to hide its brilliantly fading orange face behind a distant mountain range, I paused at the shrine of a carved spiraled stone. Although its purpose has never been determined, the impressive monument reaching for the skies is known as The Hitching Post of the Sun. Watching the sunset that day in that place was a moment of exaltation that inspired me to watch and respond to enchanting sunsets in many other places.

Speaking of the earth's orbit around the sun, retirement provides the opportunity to watch all the sun rises and sunsets you've missed through the years. It's a significant and welcome change after a long life of reporting in at 8:00 and clocking out at 5:00. Retirement is clocking out of a rigidly scheduled life. To get the benefits of a full day, I'd advise an early rise-and-shine wake-up call, but the "alarm" doesn't need to be so startling. One distinct daily pleasure is taking a mug of hot coffee to the easy chair by the window and awakened casually and peacefully by the break of a new day. Usually, after a peak of the first warming ray, I'm ready to get on with my new productive day. I recommend adopting a similar routine, because it's considerably less stressful than rushing out the door spilling coffee and weaving through ungodly traffic on the way to work.

Put Machu Picchu near the top of your list of places to see when the retirement bug begins gnawing at you. Having been asked a number of times to name my favorite place visited, I've narrowed it to Machu Picchu, the Taj Mahal in India and the Grand Canyon. Watching the sun rise or set at Machu Picchu didn't surpass the occasion when its rise cast a soft veil over the Taj Mahal. Having visited and hiked in the Grand Canyon on seven different occasions, three of my adult children and I watched three sunrises and sunsets from different vantage points during our 19-mile backpacking trip from the north rim to the south. After climbing up the steep trail the last day, we paused to watch the sun set behind the rim and cast its last ray on a most gratifying and glorious day, making it certainly one of my favorite places. Of all the sunrises and sunsets I've witnessed, the ones at Mt. Everest resembled the lights that must be shining in Heaven.

Either before or after going on an excursion, I'm often asked if I knew any of the other participants. Too often, friends and acquaintances hesitate pursuing such adventures without the familiarity and reassurance of going with someone they know. No, I didn't know any of the other participants and little or nothing about them except their names and addresses after receiving final trip information, the itinerary and trip roster. It's like going into the military where you're more-or-less forced to make friends with the guys sleeping with you in a communal foxhole.

Indeed, a group of fellow travelers who are diverse in cultures, backgrounds and experiences are a most interesting type, and those forming a group quickly become friends. Several have remained friends through ensuing years. Within every group, mutual dependency soon develops and bonds are securely formed as supporting and encouraging each other is essential. When joined together going up and down a mountain, one's life is literally in another's hands. It's not fun unless you have utmost trust in those holding the other end of your rope. To see the sites was often challenging, demanding and difficult, but the human associations and connections provided another dimension, which equaled or surpassed the initial goals. The presence of other real people sharing your adventures is truly a gift, as are the natural wonders everywhere.

After the initial meeting and greeting of a group of total strangers in places such as Bangkok, New Delhi or Kathmandu, a cohesive team must begin taking form. It's like a team with a coach and players eager and willing to play the game and, if necessary, sacrifice for the common good. Your roommate and tent mate for the next month better be a nice guy. I've shared crowded tents with an 18-year-old, a particle physicist and a farmer from Tasmania. Of the hundreds of fellow travelers on the projects, excursions and journeys, the number of obnoxious or arrogant misfits encountered can be counted on a two-fingered hand. Your new bosom friends come from varied backgrounds and different cultures, have wide educational and work experiences and are exceptionally enthusiastic and interesting people. It's a process of combining a group of diverse people with the common goal—experiencing and mutually sharing a new and exciting adventure with other venturesome people.

Without question, a team could not function without those who provide support. Porters, aides, servants and Sherpa's are indispensable to the success of long, arduous trips in the wild. Sherpas live in the Himalayan area of Nepal. They primarily serve and assist trekkers and mountain climbers in that area. Perhaps Edmund Hillary would not have been the first to summit Mt. Everest in 1954 without the loyal support of his Sherpa, Tensing Norgay. For a few dollars per day, they carry heavy packs in all kinds of weather and over rugged terrain in high elevations. They carry these packs wearing shoes which often consist of whatever they can find to wrap around their feet. Unless the temperature is near freezing or below, some of them, who are relatively small in stature, but exceptionally strong individuals, carry heavy loads barefoot over the roughest terrain.

In all my journeys and exploits, many of those who worked and guided, those simple folks who served and led the way, became friends. A lack of a common language was not a barrier in understanding and appreciating the caring, generosity and humanity of those who could never do enough. I worked, struggled and sacrificed to see the wondrous sites, but never could have reached the summits or the goals without those humble people offering their strength and giving me the courage and will to follow.

Pertemba, an older gentle and kind Sherpa, led me to the summit of Kala Patar above the base camp at the south face of Mt. Everest in Nepal. In four-foot snow, Paljour helped us cross over the 17, 500-foot Kanji La pass in Ladakh. Camel Man from Tajikistan led us to the advanced base camp on K2. Amelio kept me safe when I climbed to the summit of Pyramide Blanca in Bolivia. A photographer in India followed me around for three days. I will not forget him and the many other generous, humble and noble people I have met. Ang Porba and I spent a day wandering up and above the base at the north face of Mt. Everest in Tibet. This was a day I described as, "a grand day in my life."

After the project in Peru, which was prior to retirement and all my other trips, I came away with two distinct impressions and insights. The experience was an introduction to the possibilities of going beyond the expected bounds of a conventional and normal life to a beautiful, exciting world with vast, varied and limitless opportunities. In addition, it was an introduction to new associations with other people who were outside the realm of my somewhat limited and homogeneous social circle.

At Chacha Bomba, we marveled at our unique surroundings and talked about many other intriguing and exotic places throughout the world. Being a novice traveler, I listened to the stories and accounts of other group members, most of whom had taken other trips to exotic places. Many of the conversations included, "You must see this or that, or do this or that." Those thoughts usually pass when reality clicks in with the realization that various limitations, family responsibilities and an inadequate retirement nest egg prohibit our taking off to see the world. Nonetheless, the thought implanted—maybe someday.

I was particularly attracted to and fascinated by the high mountains formidably surrounding our quaint little site beside the roaring Urubamba River. I could only wonder how anyone could ever climb to the top of those peaks where the clouds linger! We had taken a couple of hikes partially up the side of a mountain or two. The higher you go, the better the view. Maybe I'd get the chance to go up there—part way—some day.

One of our group members had been in the Peace Corps in Africa and had spent some time in mountainous areas. One of her hobbies was photographing wild flowers, and her vacations were spent in places where they grow. She said the most beautiful wild flowers were found on the sides of mountains. We talked about the mountains and I explained to her that I hoped to see the highest ones someday. She said, "I'll send a book you must read."

The Snow Leopard by Peter Mathiessen hooked me. His book is an account of how Mathiessen and acclaimed scientist George Schaller tracked the rare and elusive snow leopard in the Himalayas. His descriptions of the rugged and spectacular terrain in the highest mountain range in the world were captivating. In addition, the accounts of the mystical places where the Buddhist monks chanted and meditated in their quaint and secluded caves and monasteries inspired me to go and have a look. Two years later, I stood in a secluded Buddhist monastery, hidden up a mountain, and listened to the chanting, songs and prayers. When I met Mr. Mathiessen a few years later, I explained he was responsible for my wandering over that part of the world on four different occasions.

Remember "Climb Every Mountain" from "The Sound of Music?" It was written for retirees. When you were working, about the only climbing you did was up the make-a-living ladder. Climbing with your children up on a horse on a merry-go-round does not count. To have a happy and fulfilling life during retirement, you don't have to do crazy things like attach ropes to your body or sleep in a tent with a glacier for a mattress. There is a summit at the end of any worthwhile goal, and the satisfaction of accomplishment provides a feeling like no other. Synonyms for the word summit are apex, climax, crescendo, crown, culmination, peak, pinnacle and ultimate. Who says we older folks can't peak to a climax?

I'm still up there. Upon reaching the top, there is a part of you that will never come down. Another part descends, ready to assault another summit. Mountain climbing terms are explicit. Assault is a rather harsh and forceful term, but that's what you should do even during retirement. Set a lofty goal, go after it with enthusiasm and give it your all.

In one's latter years, our physical capacities and capabilities obviously begin declining, but I've discovered there's a re-charging mechanism that extends one beyond normal or expected limits. I never cease to be amazed at the capacity of the physical body, even at an advanced age. Obviously, one needs good health, good fortune and good luck. I've been blessed with all three.

The age factor is a factor, but only in the sense that they who fret and worry about getting old will get there sooner. Wearing out is a reality, but worn-out is final. It wears me out thinking about it, so I'll move on to the next chapter.

CHAPTER 2

I'M RICHER THAN HE IS

❖ ❖ ❖

After setting a lofty goal, I met a man in Ladakh who claimed he was richer than I am. You met the man where? A few years ago, National Geographic ran a feature article about "Ladakh-The Last Shangri La." It is, but it's an isolated, remote and seldom visited place. The beautiful mountainous land is located in the Karakorum mountain range above the northern tip of India and borders the southwestern tip of China near the eastern border of Afghanistan. You can get there from here and travel through it, but you will have to walk. William O. Douglas, a former Supreme Court Justice and an adventurer, was one of the early travelers to take an extensive excursion through the area. An account of his adventure, *Beyond the High Himalayas*, was published in 1952. The following passage is his description of the area:

"There will be memories of the moon turning glaciers to gold. Pieces of old Tibetan love songs will come floating down a canyon already drenched with loneliness. Drums once more will beat in such a frenzied rhythm that one will want to cast off convention, join the natives, and jump and swirl in a mad exciting dance. Miles of snow-capped peaks will suddenly appear far above the earth as quickly and as magically as they came. There will be the sweet voice of a lovely girl singing of love under a poplar tree in a tiny garden of a village. Once more, the wind will whine off 25,000-foot peaks, carrying the sting of sleet on its wings. Acres of poppies once more will stretch as far as the eye can see. And perhaps the loveliest of all will be the sounds of a flute—a flute blown by a lonely shepherd high on the crags, a flute whose music sounds like falling water."

I've heard Tibetan love songs like pure falling water echoing through the canyons. I've watched thick clouds break and fade away, uncovering the highest peaks. To see the tops strains the eye, but such wondrous views both rouse and soothe the soul. I've heard the bells from yak trains and watched glaciers turn from bluish-white to gold. In high and secluded places, I've heard Buddhist monks chant and sing, praising the passion of a compassionate life.

Wealth can be measured in a number of ways. I became a richer man, because I felt the stings of sleet and heard the sweetest music echoing from the highest canyon walls. My initial opportunity to see and experience the sights described above only intensified my desire to return to where miles of snow-capped peaks suddenly appear far above this earth.

After captivated by the book *The Snow Leopard,* I was anxious to see the mountains and particularly Mt. Everest. Knowing I would have a month's vacation during the summer of 1989, I investigated ways to go. However, from June to October the monsoons sweep north from the Indian Ocean breaking against the high Himalayas that run east and west for nearly 2,000 miles. The southern slopes are wet and soggy where a journey to those mountains normally begins. Since the heavy summer rains do not drench the northern ranges in most parts of the Karakorum, I chose to travel to Ladakh.

After a long, arduous day trekking through the beautifully serene and majestic mountains in Ladakh, our group stopped to set up camp for the night. We had not seen any other people during the day, but noticed activity just up ahead. Smoke was rising from the top of a small hut made from rocks stacked haphazardly on top of one another. The makeshift roof was layered with branches, twigs and dirt. We then observed a large flock of sheep and goats herded down a mountainside. Two young men and their dog were coaxing their flock into a flimsy corral near the hut. Hashmat, one of our guides from India, began talking to the eldest young man, who invited us over to their hut for tea later that evening.

After our meal, three of our group accepted the invitation and walked the short distance to their hut. The other members of our group were pooped and nestled themselves into their sleeping bags for the night. When we entered the crudely constructed hut through a small opening covered by an animal skin, a young lady threw a straw mat down on the dirt so we could sit. She then resumed stirring their dinner in a pot boiling over a hearth in the center of the hut. The smoke from the fire burned my eyes as it rose up and out through the flimsy roof. Four straw mats with animal skins piled on top for beds were scattered around the side of their igloo-sized summer home. It gets very cold at night up in the mountains, even in summertime, and brutally cold in the winters.

Hashmat and the young man talked as the young lady poured tea in cups we had taken with us. The young man, about 20, his younger brother, about 14, and 2 sisters, I would guess about 18 and eight had spent nearly a month taking their herd from the lowlands to the hills and mountains to graze the lush vegetation at their summer camp. In early fall, it would require nearly another month to take their flock back down the valley and home. We had sheep back when I was growing up in Kentucky and lived in the hills. However, our hills weren't as high and steep as theirs were, and we couldn't afford a summer camp.

They had brought sacks of barley and rice, spices and salt. The goats and sheep provided all the milk for yogurt, butter and cheese they would need. On a large rock outside their summer home, cheese cured and ripened in the sun. The young man proudly showed us his butter churn, but the churn we used when I was growing up on the farm was never used to mix butter and salt with our tea.

After the young lady mixed the ingredients in the churn, tea was served. It was a very hot mixture of salt, sheep's milk and tea, but if there was any tea in the concoction, I couldn't taste it. I sipped slowly as Hashmat and the young shepherd talked. It was a cozy, warm and secure place, but eliminate the smoke, drink some tea without the butter and salt, and it would have been a perfect evening.

In later trips to the Himalayas, I was "forced" to drink tea—yak butter tea—on numerous occasions, and forced to drink it from cups that, undoubtedly, had never been washed. On one occasion, an old gentleman poured a small amount of water in my cup, and, using his grimy finger as a rag, swirled it around the cup, poured it out, then poured it full of the hot, thick stuff and graciously handed it to me. Many people in that part of the world live on yak butter tea and barley. Yak butter tea is brewed with yak butter, a hearty dose of salt and a limited amount of tea. The heated ingredients are sloshed and blended in a churn and then poured into cups. Despite holding my breath when bringing a cup to my lips, I never developed a taste for the highly nutritious mix. To be congenial and appreciative, I later learned how to fake it. Timing was essential. When no one was watching, I'd cautiously throw the rancid liquid on the ground, then periodically lift the cup to my lips, and take deep swallows of air.

As the conversation over tea continued, Hashmat occasionally paused to relay information about the family and their story. I interrupted at one point and asked him to tell the young man that I grew up on a farm with 110 sheep. There was a pause while the young man thought for a moment before responding to Hashmat, who then looked over at me.

"He said to tell you he has almost 250 sheep and goats and is 'much richer than you are.'"

The next morning, we packed up and prepared for another day's trek under a clear blue sky in crisp pure air. When we passed by the hut, the two sisters were outside preparing for the day. The two young shepherds and their dog were getting ready to take the flock to fresher grass higher up the mountain. I stopped and gave the smaller sister a pack of gum. As the others huddled around, I tried explaining it was chewing gum, and pantomimed tearing it open, putting a piece in my mouth and chewing it. They smiled as I, now a richer man, waved and walked away that beautiful day.

Finally, we're at the subject that touches our hearts down to the core. Yes, it's money. How are you going to retire without the dough? Unless filthy rich, how are you going to travel the world and take tea with shepherds? If you were born rich, had a wealthy uncle who loved you or lucked out and struck it rich some other way, no problem. If you start life with little means and the homefolks have little to give other than sending you off with, "We love you and don't forget to write," you then have to make it on your own. However, there is a way. If you are an average, middle class, relatively sensible and at least half-intelligent, healthy human being, there is a way.

When discussing or giving presentations about my trips, I'm frequently asked questions pertaining to the cost. Although not explicitly stating it, I've been asked indirectly, "Where did you get the money?" I made it legally. If you want to go to Ladakh after retiring, here are my money rules:

1. *Start the piggy bank early and keep it going.*
2. *Drive used cars.*
3. *Buy only what you need.*

Before explaining piggy bank and used-car financial dynamics, it should be noted that 80 million Americans—the Baby Boomers—will be retiring during the next 20 years. A 65-year old man can expect to live to age 82, and a woman can expect to live to 85. It's not fair for a woman to live three years longer. Life expectancy is increasing and many retirees are living well beyond those ages. I have three friends in their mid 90's who are as sharp as the tacks we used to nail linoleum to our floors. One 95-year-old friend dates. He's not dated, but dates a lovely 89-year-old lady. One 96-year-old does her taxes. Hope is eternal.

With such an astoundingly large demographic group, it's not surprising that there are an exhaustive number of published books about retirement. In addition, there are numerous other sources of information available, including newspaper and magazine articles, retirement magazines, "senior" websites, TV programs and documentaries, discs, and government publications.

Need a book on if, why, when, where and how to retire? There are scads of books on the subject available from Amazon. The books, print and web materials cover all aspects of retirement—finances, health, where to live, what to do and how to do it. There are books and information available on second careers, employment including part time, volunteering and strengthening your spiritual life in preparation for the streets paved with gold. In this age of information overload, we're swamped. The variety and quantity of materials about retirement is no exception. Search the web, select the materials and if you read 5 percent of the stuff, it will be like carrying a 142-pound pack through Ladakh.

If work is a necessity or a passion, you might want to scan *Working after Retirement for Dummies.* Dummy me, shortly after retirement I painted the inside of my house, because the paint was peeling from the walls. Since then, I try to avoid any work associated with lawn grooming, garage re-arrangement so I can drive the car in and situations where I have to stir paint.

One of the seminal books for future retirees was published in 1980, *The Graying of America: Retirement and Why You Can't Afford It* by James Jorgenson. He addressed why the retirement plans in place at that time would not work for the large numbers of future retirees, those 80 million of us graying to the extent we've been called America's "silver tsunami." Jorgenson's premise was that the limited and deficient pension plans available at that time, primarily Social Security, did not provide sufficient resources for much more than a meager existence, if that. Although his intent was not to predict doom and gloom, he stressed the urgent need to create a retirement system that would provide adequate financial security.

Since then, better plans and programs have been devised, adopted and institutionalized. Consequently, the prospering economy these past 20-25 years has been relatively rewarding for most of us provided we did not experience some type of financial calamity or a circumstance that wiped us out. You can review the literature and read everything from *How to Retire Rich* to *Getting Started in a Financially Secure Retirement* to *America's Best Low-Tax Retirement Towns.*

Most retirees, but certainly not all, now have three or four separate plans or programs to assist in providing financial security during our graying golden years including Social Security, company pension plans, IRAs and an optional piggy bank or individual savings plan. I began inserting coins in my piggy bank early on, which eventually provided the funds to finance occasions like having tea with Princess Diana in London. The tea she served wasn't brewed with yak butter, thank you.

In brief, this is my money story as it relates to how I was fortunate enough to drink yak butter tea and eat tsampa (barley) with Ladakhis, Nepalis and Tibetans.

I was born in the hills of Kentucky, half way between Short Creek and Locust Grove near Slick Ridge, which is one hollow south of Hog Ridge. I was born at 12:00 noon on Sunday, July 15, 1934 in a house built soon after the Civil War. The day was one of the hottest and driest days on record and smack dab in the middle of the Great Depression. You can't start life off much lower than that.

We owned our farm and grew what we ate, but from my earliest days, I remember how my grandfather worried about having enough at the end of the year to make the mortgage payment and pay the taxes. There were times when he nearly lost the farm and everything. I grew up understanding that we only purchased what we had to have. With plenty of milk, butter, eggs, chicken, beef, pork, lamb, the garden in summer and the shelves in the cellar stacked with home-canned fruits and vegetables for winter, we had plenty to eat. Elmer's country store down the road provided sugar, coffee, baking powder and a few other items, and if you were an honest man, they would write it on your tab. When the tobacco crop sold, you'd settle up.

Only two of the 20 members of my high school graduating class went to college. Morgan High School was located on the banks of the South Licking River, which flowed through a scenic valley nestled below the rolling hills in north central Kentucky. Most Morgan Raider graduates remained on the farms surrounding the beautiful valley, and made a decent, respectable and modest living from the land. The number of my extended family members (my mother had 95 first cousins) who attended college could be counted on one hand.

Transylvania College in Lexington, Kentucky offered me a $200 scholarship. With money like that, how could I refuse? Transylvania is the oldest college west of the Allegheny Mountains and the 16th college in the U.S. Thomas Jefferson helped found the college in 1790. When I went there in the fall of 1952, my assets consisted of the $200 scholarship, one heifer calf, five sheep and a half-acre of tobacco. When I sold the tobacco crop just before Christmas that year, half the profit went to my landlord and grandfather, Frank Marquette, who raised me. The other half was barely enough to enroll for the second semester my freshman year.

Yes, I know. Tobacco smoke will kill you, but at that time in Kentucky, many families survived on the proceeds of their tobacco crop. You can't eat it, but the meager profit from its sale at the end of the year provided the means to my continuing and finishing college.

Basketball was important to me, and I made the Transylvania Pioneer team. My coach, C. M. Newton, who at 24 was the youngest college coach in the nation, had played for the legendary coach Adolph Rupp at the University of Kentucky. C. M. later

became a successful coach at the University of Ala-
bama, Vanderbilt University and athletic director at
the University of Kentucky. He was quite a guy, an
inspiration and always eager to help his boys. Learning that it had been a lean year farming, he took me
to see about a campus job and explained, "Dr. Crawford, this boy's tobacco crop went through a drought
this summer and he doesn't want to sell his heifer
calf just yet. Can you find a part-time job for him to
help him stay in school?"

Dr. Crawford, who was lying back in his comfortable chair staring at the ceiling with his feet propped
up on his desk, slowly sat up. He looked me directly
in the eye and asked, "What can he do, plow?"

"Yes, I can and anything else you want me to do,"
I said. I got a job cleaning the gym and locker rooms
and made my grades, which were significantly below
making the dean's list, but slightly higher than the
dreaded probation list.

During a class in the early part of my second year,
I became distracted. A student with long, blonde
hair sauntered into one of my classes and plopped
down at the desk in front of me. The long blonde
hair soon began interfering with my education. At
times strands of it would slither down over my book
causing my eyes for reading to remain unfocused.
Say it's literature and "The Rape of the Lock" by
Alexander Pope. You're trying to follow the meta-
phors and rhyme schemes, but strands of golden
ringlets obscure the page. Her hair changed my life.
Vera and I married because of love, and because I'd

heard two could live as cheaply as one. Two can, but not six, as we discovered a few years later when Dani, Tim and twins Clint and Curt were born. One advantage, though, of having twins in December is you get two more tax deductions for that year, which saves you enough to feed them.

All able-bodied men were drafted into the military back in the 50's. If enrolled in college and making a C average, you could be deferred for four years before your military obligation. Upon graduation, I put the diploma in a drawer and put on a silly little white hat. Navy pay back then was about one-fourth minimum wage, so I learned to use one-fourth the amount of toothpaste I'd normally put on a brush. After protecting our country for two years, I was honorably discharged and financially broke.

After tossing the funny little white hat in another drawer in 1958, I went from rags to riches. My first job after military service paid $3,550 per year. I taught English, health and physical education, helped manage the library and coached junior high and high school basketball and baseball. My wife's first job paid $3,250 to teach high school math and physics. We suddenly became so rich, I bought a $25 savings bond each month. The bonds and other savings plans during the next 33 years financed trips to Europe, Ladakh, Siberia, Peru, Tibet, Ecuador, Nepal, Bolivia, India, China, Argentina, the Soviet Union and seven trips to the Grand Canyon.

I was appointed principal of Pendleton County (Kentucky) High School at age 27 in 1962. The school had recently become the consolidated high school of my home county. The consolidation included my alma mater, Morgan High School. With four young children, Vera had an around-the-clock job without pay. My $6,142 salary financed only the basics—clothing, food, shelter and four pieces of bubble gum on the weekends.

One of the last things a 27-year-old thinks about is a retirement plan. However, I was thinking and very concerned about how I would ever have the resources to provide the opportunity for my children to attend college. Attaining that goal was my number-one priority.

Education was my life. My college experience was a dream fulfilled. A school building was my second home. My grandfather, who raised me on the farm, was a believer in education and inspired me to continue mine. His formal education in the 1890's took him through the fifth grade, and he realized what might have been attained had he had the opportunity. He was a highly intelligent man, very active in community affairs and served in the Kentucky state legislature.

His father, my great-grandfather, John Julius Marquette, came from Germany with his family when he was seven. He marched with General Sherman to the sea during the Civil War, and upon returning to the hills and the farm, he married and built the house where I grew up. After marriage, his wife, Nancy, taught him to read. As my grandfather tells the story, once his father learned to read, he would not stop. Often he would read all through the night. During the day, he'd take his six boys to the hay, corn and tobacco fields and put them to work. He would take along some books, sit under a shade tree and read all day while the boys worked. After being self-educated, he served in the Kentucky legislature before the turn of the 20th century.

On our farm, we had two small houses, or they were more like shacks, back on a ridge where our tenant farmers (sharecroppers) lived. Through the years, several different families moved in and out, and most of the adult tenants were illiterate. Although their children went to school sporadically, few became functionally literate. I worked in the fields every day with those humble souls, and learned to talk their talk with little reference to the written word. In 2007, I published my first novel about a tenant farm family struggling to survive during the Great Depression.

With this background, I realized the importance of "schooling" and formal education from those who had little or none. From the day my children were born, I was determined they would have the opportunity to attend college, if they so desired. During the early years of my career, providing the essentials for the family was a break-even proposition. However, when salaries in education began increasing somewhat, Vera returned to teaching and our financial situation improved. There was a little extra each month, and I began to save and invest. In the 1970's, the federal government initiated a tax-sheltered program, which eventually could be converted later into an IRA. Professional educators were permitted to save and invest a sizeable sum in the program.

I provided the necessities for my family while living comfortably on a bit less. If the take home pay was around $1,000 per month like in the 70's, I learned to make it on $900. The other $100 went into the piggy bank. If you don't "see" it, you won't spend it. Of course, it was much easier to save before credit cards came along, and what you saw was a bill at the end of the month you couldn't pay. As take-home pay increases, the savings should increase. Take home $3,000 and invest $300. Do this for 25-35 years, and you'll be as amazed as Albert Einstein was. When asked what the most powerful force on earth was, he replied, "Compound interest."

To compound your retirement fund, you should drive used cars, the kind that little old ladies drive only to the store on Saturday and church on Sunday. Bought my first car, a 1940 Plymouth Road King, in 1952 for $235 and sold it in 1954 for $75. Bought a 1950 Studebaker in 1954 for $510 and traded it in 1959 for a 1953 Plymouth and $300. From 1952 through 2009—57 years—I've owned 19 different vehicles at a total cost of $71,817, including the used cars Vera and I now drive. The 1996 Toyota Camry provides excellent transportation around town, and the low-mileage 2002 Honda Odyssey should last several more years. I know people who spend $71,817 every few years on brand new cars because they like a new-car smell.

I'd be lousy rich if each of my four children hadn't wrecked at least one of my cars. The twins turned a small Datsun station wagon over in a ditch, got out, pushed it back up on its four wheels and drove home. I didn't throw a raving fit, because, although the car was dented and scratched, they weren't. I'm glad I didn't keep records on body-shop repairs, or I'd be depressed like we were during the Great Depression.

Being frugal and thrifty, or the type who is "so tight he squeaks," does not necessarily mean you abuse your children. When my kids reached about age four, to avoid waste, they had to eat the foods they put on their plates, OK, almost everything. When my kids were seven, they were instructed never to expect me to buy them a car. Drive by a high school parking lot today, but don't pull in because you won't find a parking place.

Compound interest is a powerful force. Without "seeing" the money invested in the college fund for my kids, the amount grew substantially through the years. I was able to pay room, board and tuition for all four, and they all attained college degrees.

As the investments continued growing, I was fortunate enough to establish an education fund for assisting each of my five grandchildren. There were conditions and requirements attached in order for them to qualify. I invested $2,000 in various mutual stock funds for each grandchild soon after they were born. Some of the funds grew at a faster rate while others didn't perform as well. One fund invested in a health care mutual fund grew from $2,000 to over $70,000 twenty years later. Two grandchildren have completed their education and two are currently in college with one to go. Without my assistance, two of them would not have had the means to continue their education.

When I retired in 1991, monthly payouts from Social Security and the Teacher's Retirement Pension Fund were adequate in meeting our basic living expenses. Travel was limited, however, to trips to the grocery store. The savings fund established years earlier to be used for our children's education had not only accomplished its purpose, but had not been depleted and it continued to grow. When our IRAs began paying out a few years later, I had the resources to travel throughout the world.

Investing in the stock market certainly has its risks as evidenced by the recent 2000 and 2008 bursting bubbles. Returns in the mid-1980's through the 1990's were considerable. Then the technology stocks bubble burst with a decline of around 20-25 percent. It took about three years to regain those losses and the market took off again until the housing mortgage bubble burst in 2008, with individual losses of 30 to 50 percent. It was and is devastating to all those who have IRAs and other retirement plans invested in stocks. It was particularly devastating to those who planned to retire in a year or two. I took significant losses. My regret is that I didn't switch my stock funds into much safer bond funds at some point when the market continued declining.

The sharp decline undoubtedly forced time line changes and delays for those planning to retire in the next few years. An early 2009 national survey asking the question, "Have the stock market losses caused you to postpone your retirement?" indicated the following: 32 percent said it won't change the date, 32 percent said it would delay retirement from two to five years and 36 percent indicated they would never be able to retire. It's a very unfortunate circumstance.

The market did make a comeback. It always has and will, won't it? From March 19 through October 9, 2002, the S&P 500 declined 33 percent. Then it gained 120 percent the next five years or approximately 24 percent per year. Who knows how long it will take to recover from the steep decline in 2008? And how many future retirees will hesitate or refuse to invest in the stock market again? You work hard all your life and within a month or two, half your life savings has disappeared.

Saving and investing is a long-term proposition, and there are strategies to reduce risk. Due to stock market volatility (particularly the 2008 debacle), you may be stock-market gun shy. Investing in bonds and treasuries will produce approximately a 5 percent gain over time, and the results will be substantial. A combination of stocks and bonds or some type of balanced fund is a more conservative approach and less risky.

I'm not a financial expert—there aren't any—but the best investment advice I can offer is to buy low and sell high. That's what they all say. No, my advice is to save something—any amount—and start early and keep it going. A 10-20-40 plan works well. Save $20 per week for 40 years invested at a 10.5 percent return (the approximate historical return of the stock market) and you will have over a $700,000 nest egg. If traveling, hiking, trekking, climbing and running are not in your retirement plan, you can take several cruises around the world or buy a coastal condo and medium-sized yacht for $700,000.

Or, try the 10-20-30-plan. If you save only $10 per month for 30 years at 20 percent interest, you'll have a million dollars. Obviously, getting a 20 percent return for 30 years is practically impossible. No, it isn't. Warren Buffet is one of the best all-time investors ever. His Berkshire-Hathaway Fund averaged 21.1 percent from 1965 through 2007. Had I invested only $1,000 in his fund in 1965, I'd now have $4,301,232. Oh, well.

Save something for retirement, and you won't regret it. You work for 35 years and then have fun for perhaps 35 more years or more. Drink one less diet Coke each day and save one extra dollar each day for 40 years at 10.5 percent and you'd have over $250,000, which will finance several mountain climbing expeditions.

If you retire soon and haven't saved, it's too late. However, your offspring might finally learn something from you. Tell them to save a dollar each day, or tell them about a 10-20-30 or 10-20-40 plan. When I explained to my 27-year-old grandson what a 10-20-30 plan could do, he told me he could save more than $10 per week, and he is.

A former co-worker and friend's financial situation was similar to mine. When I retired rather early, he asked how I afforded it. I explained that I had saved and invested all I could through the years. His response, "Wish I had done that." Bill is still working.

Say you're around age 50 with 10 years to go and haven't saved much. You can't see much of the world on $5 per day. Typically, most retirees do want to have the resources to do the "normal" things sane retirees do. Perhaps take the European tour, meander through the west, a month or two in the sunny south during winter and the time and necessities for hobbies or an avocation.

A friend in her early forties asked, "But what if we haven't saved?" If you have 10 or 15 years to go, start now. If receiving a $200 raise per month, put at least $100 or all of it away. In most cases, it's not that difficult learning to live on what you've been living on. If you're practically broke at 62 and plan to retire at 63, call a family meeting. Explain to your kids and grandkids that you threw your piggy bank away, but demand they keep theirs. Don't they listen to you?

My month-long trip to Ladakh in 1989 cost less than $4,000. That same type trip now would cost around

$10,000. It was an incredible journey and worth every penny. It was challenging, exciting and demanding, particularly when we approached Leh, which is the only sizeable town in Ladakh, but they wouldn't let us in, because Pakistan and India had resumed conflict. The only thing we could do then was adjust to the circumstance, and it worked out. Retirement is also a big adjustment, and some people adjust the next day.

CHAPTER 3

I ADJUSTED THE NEXT DAY

❖ ❖ ❖

Retirement is a major adjustment. It is especially difficult when adjusting to an atmosphere where your oxygen is reduced in half. I retired on a Monday, went home, packed a couple of duffle bags and flew out on Saturday for Lukla, Nepal. Fifteen days later, I was gasping for air above the base camp at Mt. Everest.

I'd wanted to begin retirement by getting away, so I flew halfway around the world, which is about as far away as you can get. It's a long way to go to see a mountain, but that's what I wanted to do. When giving the "thank-you" speech at a retirement party, retirees don't say, "Good, now I get to do what I don't want to do."

Looking back on my career in education, I have no regrets. Obviously, there were those times when I would have done a number of things differently, but I enjoyed working with high-school-age young people, although, at times, they can drive you nuts. I was 27 in 1962, when appointed principal of Pendleton County High School in Kentucky where I grew up. The times were much different then. It was a time when, if a kid was spanked at school, there would be another spanking waiting for him at home. I actually spanked high school boys the first couple of years during my career. It was expected, and the community approved. Lawyers then were busy with other crimes. On very rare occasions, a grouchy, old lady teacher would take pleasure in called upon to whack a girl.

Corporal punishment bothered me, but, in those days, that is the way it was. If a principal wasn't tough, he didn't last long. Elza was the last kid I spanked. He was not malicious, but just always into something like pulling ponytails or trying to get spit-balls to stick on ceilings. When he was sent to my office for the nth time, I said, "OK, Elza, I warned you and I'm tired of seeing you in here so it's three licks. Take your billfold out of your pocket and put you elbows on the desk." He knew it was coming, but I was certainly having second thoughts about this "tried-and-true" method. With the paddle drawn back, I hesitated.

"Elza, what would your mother think of what you've been doing?"

"My mother's dead."

"Well, then what would your father think?"

"He's dead, too."

Although I didn't know it at the time, they were. Elza got three of the lightest licks you could imagine, and then we talked about the situation and came to an understanding. When Elza realized I was genuinely interested in him, he began shaping up. We became buddies in a sense, and he stopped driving his teachers up to the ceiling where the spitballs were stuck.

School disciplinarians are expected to punish kids. Obviously, corporal punishment wasn't the answer then, or now. Suspension or expulsion isn't either, although with the hard core, there's no other choice. In later years, I often assigned a trouble-maker, who, in most cases, was personally troubled, a 500-word theme titled "My Family." Talk about revelations. After reading the theme, we'd have a conference and talk about their behaviors and how best to correct them. Many of the students would pour out their hearts in the themes. It was an opportunity for them to tell someone their concerns, worries and feelings about, "My dad's OK until he gets half-drunk most every night," or "I don't trust the man who moved in with Mom."

Not many young people living in a dysfunctional home will do well in school. After reading the accounts of many students' situations, I'd often think that, under the circumstances, this particular student was performing much better than I would in such a situation. The themes revealed everything from a stepfather sexually abusing his stepdaughter to a mother shacking up with a neighbor. A student worrying about what conflicts will erupt at home tonight cannot concentrate on diagramming sentences in English class. I have a file drawer filled with "My Family" themes. There is enough material in that drawer for another book.

Through the years, I confiscated stink bombs, knives and guns. I've stashed enough cheap vodka and enough marijuana to send me up for a year. I've removed drunk and stoned students from science labs and choir rooms during rehearsals of Christmas carols. You name it, and I've dealt with everything imaginable, except rape and murder. Students do find ways to disappear in dark closets or vacant rooms to play around. And, a teacher can do things with a student on a wrestling mat during a planning period in a gym locker. It happens. Gay teachers write "love" notes to boys, which mothers find. It happens.

If a high school has 1,000 students and five percent have problems and are problems, there are 50 students each day sleeping in class, skipping school or smoking something in the restroom. The most frustrating aspect is that there is simply not enough time to properly deal with it all.

It's very rewarding to turn a kid around and know you've helped put a young life back on track. There are many individual challenges in any school, and if schools were adequately staffed, we'd see a difference. There is never enough time to do what should be done. In addition to counseling and disciplining students, supervising and evaluating teachers, working on curriculum and schedules, you have to patrol the parking lot, restrooms, hallways and concealed places where boys and girls rendezvous. You try enforcing a strict hands-off policy, and they'll rub other parts of their bodies. If lunch hour is not what it's like in Hell, it's the next level above. French fries are used as missiles and plastic catsup packets as squirt guns.

Dealing with problem students requires time and patience and a student who understands that you do care. They can read you. When a troubled student realizes you have a genuine interest in their welfare, it's like seeing a flower begin to bloom. Getting the parents (or parent or step-parent or significant other or foster parent or a grandparent or another relative) involved is an important part of the process, but, again, it's most time consuming. Most parents are supportive, but many have no answers either, and hope the school can correct the problem.

Mrs. Johnson sent a note: "You need to look at Robert's T-shirt." Robert was a very bright sophomore who would never violate a rule. He went on to get a doctorate in medieval philosophy. When he entered my office, I focused on his shirt, but saw nothing unusual. As he came closer, I noticed tiny words splotched all over the shirt. Upon closer examination, Robert was communicating to me, and the world, "F*#k You." I called his mother. When she arrived, I asked her to look at his shirt. "Yes, I know. I bought it for him, because we want him to be more assertive and learn to express his individuality."

It was the first day after the holiday break. Usually, that day is the calmest day of the year, because the kids are like zombies after two weeks of parties, all-night TV and sleeping until three in the afternoon. The students drifted to their classrooms after the first bell. Three minutes later, I received a note from Mrs. Rose, "Please come and take Jason out of my class, because he's drunk."

Jason explained things hadn't gone very well during the break. His parents fought, and would probably divorce, and he simply could not face going back to school. After driving to the parking lot, he sat in his car agonizing whether to go inside and remembered the bottle under the seat. A few swigs might help provide the courage. I mustered the courage all those years without nipping, but if I'd had a bottle….

Cheerleaders don't usually drink, especially during a game when they're flipping all over the floor in skirts one-half inch below the you-know-what. They do support the team and support hunk athletes in various ways. Five thousand fans packed the gym for the big game with our bitter rival. I had worked very hard to promote sportsmanship so our cheerleaders decided to be perfect hosts and prepared a nice hospitality room for the opposing cheerleaders. Early the next Monday morning, the bitter-rival principal called; "The brownies your cheerleaders baked for our cheerleaders contained Ex-lax and two had to go to a doctor."

All that's needed is to adopt a strict set of rules, or so I thought. On the first day of school each year, I would simply give out a booklet, somewhat briefer than the tax code, and approved by a law firm, which explained every conceivable situation regarding student behavior and the consequences of any violations. Kids are sharp. They'll find loopholes. Section II-B-3a regarding short skirts does not cover see-throughs. An editorial in the school newspaper comparing the principal's intelligence to that of a mule is covered under the free speech amendment.

I eventually reduced the rules to five, which worked better than a thick rulebook with about 130 thou-shalt-nots such as, "In the beginning, thou shalt not chew gum."

1. *Behave*
2. *Don't worry*
3. *Be happy*
4. *Do your work*
5. *Respect everyone*

"Your behavior is actually causing you to worry too much, and you need to become happier. I can explain how, if you want me to." They usually want you to.

A school should have teachers. Bus drivers deliver children, the principal welcomes them each morning and then when a bell rings the students shall go to a room and shut up. The teacher then must do something with them. What does a teacher do? No one really knows. Most teachers teach, but a few others consider themselves successful it they can keep students in a room for an hour without them harming each other.

Why am I telling you all this? God said, "All of you who have labored and are heavy laden will reap retirement milk and honey if you've been a good and faithful servant like Moses." Moses was the first to deliver e-mail from upon high, but in too many instances, the laws were considered Spam and deleted. Although Moses didn't make it to the promised land, you will, after delivering your children from bondage. Hang in there.

Generally, counselors have a student load of four to five hundred students or more. To give optimum time to all and particularly to those needing considerable help is impossible.

Some of the teachers also have social, psychological or other types of personal disorders from time to time. A teacher living in a home with tension, stress and conflict will not perform well in the classroom. Most principals will tell you they have more problems with teachers than with students. Many ineffective teachers, either unskilled, incompetent or ones with an I-don't-give-a-damn attitude, fight battles with the enemy every day. They send their problem students to the office and then blame the administrator for not resolving their problems and giving them support. Ernie is a prince in all his classes except in Algebra II when Mr. "Over My Head" Thornton turns his back to put an equation on the board.

I didn't know the good teachers were in the building until the end of the day when they stopped by to see how my day went. The great teachers not only teach the subject matter effectively, but they also see the unlimited potential in every student, and develop and inspire young people to learn and achieve at very high levels. The excellent ones help keep the world from blowing up.

One group I had to deal with were tenured teachers counting the days to retirement. They've been on the job for years but don't like kids now and probably never did. They're out there. It's like choosing to go into the ministry, but not believing in God.

Not only did I spend countless hours attempting to turn wayward students around, try turning a set-in-his-ways teacher around, or one on the verge of an emotional breakdown. One of my most difficult days ever was forcibly removing a teacher, who had gone off the deep end, from a classroom, and convincing him to let me take him to a psychiatric hospital. I arrived home after midnight.

Teaching is a very demanding and stressful profession and both mentally and physically draining. For example, high-school English teachers typically teach about 150 individual students each day with about 30 or more in each of 5 classes. A competent and professional English teacher will have 150 themes to review and grade each weekend. If not impossible, the demand is exhausting and frustrating, because a dedicated teacher soon realizes that to do the job, each day should be 48 hours duration. The majority of teachers earn every cent they're paid. Thank a teacher sometime.

Teaching, containing or entertaining 24 to 35 students in a room each hour is an awesome responsibility. If 10 or 20 of those students would rather be anywhere else in the world than in that classroom, you get the picture. A teacher has little or no time or place to take a misbehaving student aside to give counsel. "If I took Johnny out in the hall, the lid might come off in the room."

If my day happened to be somewhat uneventful, there was always the next day, hour or minute. Miss Blackburn had one of her students bring me a sealed envelope with a soft object enclosed. Her classified communiqué explained: "Somebody hung this condom on my door knob. It's a sick world." She's right, it is.

Students also have mental lapses on school buses, and very few bus drivers have had graduate courses in psychology. Most drivers can keep a bus on a road, but some have difficulty adjusting to the optical requirement of keeping one eye on the road and one on the rearview mirror. Big Fred could. One afternoon he slammed on the brakes and told Clyde to move to the front seat. Clyde told him he wasn't going to move anywhere. When Big Fred asked, "Why not?" Clyde said he didn't feel like it. So, Big Fred went back and got him in a vice-grip headlock and dragged him to the front. Clyde finally slumped down when he began turning bluish. How did I know all this? Clyde's dad called. There was no way to get Clyde's dad and Big Fred together to work it out without the police. It would require another chapter to describe the complex nature of school bus drivers.

Some of my more difficult days were dealing with the premature deaths of students. It happened every year, particularly car wrecks, but also with illnesses and other causes. A few years ago during the last period of the day, a senior girl wrote in her notebook, "I hope I never have to come to this school again." Fifteen minutes later, the car she and three other students were in hit a dump truck head on and all were killed instantly.

The most difficult days involved encounters with students who were having thoughts of running away or suicide. During my career, a number did. Perhaps my worst school day ever occurred in September, 1962, during my first year as principal. The enrollment at Pendleton County High School was about 500 students at the time. We were close-knit and like family, and I knew every student by name. The students were issued a lock for their locker, if they wanted one. Within a year or so, students realized locks were not needed. They are not necessary if you can create a trusting environment. Visitors from other schools and the public couldn't believe a school could function without locks. We did.

On that beautiful fall day, two freshman boys went home on school buses. They were from different parts of the county, had been in different elementary schools, and it was doubtful if they had yet formed a friendship or knew each other. When Bobby arrived home, he went out to an old barn and hung himself. Dan took a gun when he went to get the cows on his farm and shot himself. His parents wanted to believe it was an accident, but the circumstances did not confirm that theory. When I retrieved Bobby's belongings from his locker, he had made drawings in his notebook of a gallows. Both families and friends did not have any indication that anything was wrong.

The next afternoon our teachers met after an impossible day at school. What was there to say? I explained I didn't want anyone thinking that something we had done or failed to do contributed to this tragedy. We sat there in numbed silence, as few eyes remained dry. But you keep thinking about it, agonizing about it. Was there something more we could have done or said to help save these young lives? That's what you live with when working with young minds, hearts and souls. You can only do so much, but can't escape the thoughts and self-pressure to better understand where the severest problems are and make the effort to address them.

You see it in their faces. When Mary rushed into my office, I immediately knew something was wrong. Her expression was similar to that of Eddie's on that stormy day a few years prior. He had burst into my office and said, "Come quick, we saw a tornado passing by." The tornado began dropping softball size hail on our school and breaking skylights. The tornado killed four people two miles from our school.

Mary said, "Come quick, you need to go in the girls bathroom." As we rushed there, she told me Leah Ann was trying to hurt herself.

"I'm coming in! I'm coming in!" I shouted, but there were no other girls in the restroom. Leah Ann was fully clothed, sitting on a commode in a back stall, and trying to cut her wrists with a rusty pair of scissors.

When Leah Ann returned to school a week later, I made it a point to see her every few days. She'd smile and indicate or say, "Everything's good now." That's all you have to do every day and night, try making things good for everybody.

You might think schools are like wild jungles or zoos without cages. This is not true, although sometimes students do bring animals of various kinds to school. I once caught five chickens wandering the halls. One senior class planned to celebrate graduation by bringing a horse inside, but they selected a different animal. I heard squealing. A half-grown pig with "Class of 75" painted over his bacon slab was running loose. I picked up the pig like it was a candy wrapper and the seniors cheered and followed me through the halls as if I were a kind of pied piper. Photos were taken and an art student painted a portrait—The Principal and the Pig. It wasn't bad. You could see Picasso's influence.

I'd prefer chasing a pig through the school than 41 snakes on the loose. Raymond was creative and had never caused a problem. In the afternoons, he worked on building a house in a building trade class. It was springtime and had been raining. The lowlands around the partially constructed house were flooded, causing certain animals to come out of hibernation. Raymond noticed activity in the muddy yard. He took his gym bag outside, picked up 41 garter snakes and caught his bus back to school.

The bus arrived two minutes before the final bell, which gave him ample time to dump the snakes in the locker area.

The bell rang just as 41 snakes began slithering over the slick tile. Some were lucky and found the air vents in the lockers, hiding under coats, books or in stinky sneakers. The happy children hurried to their lockers. (I'll skip this part, because there's no way to describe it.)

Announcing a Code Red alert, I ordered the custodial staff to forget about cleaning until they had placed 41 snakes in a sealed container. To this day, 22 snakes lurk coiled somewhere in the building.

Kids are bright, great and funny. Unless having fun with them, you won't survive. Many of the rewards for your efforts come later. Jack was from a big family and his father was disabled. Jack was so cocky, arrogant and obnoxious; you wanted to choke him. He was one of the hopeless cases, but somehow finally managed to graduate. Four years later, he stopped by to tell me he was beginning his student teaching.

Phillip lived at the end of a gravel road. His father, who eked out a living on a hill farm, gave him a calf each year so he would have some money in case he wanted to go to college. After school, I would occasionally go to the gym and play basketball with Phillip and other members of our team. It was a good way to unwind, and the kids appreciated me playing ball with them. Phillip graduated in 1962. His record was not sterling, but we knew he was very intelligent with considerable potential. He wanted to continue playing basketball so he went to a small college. After a few weeks, the coach advised it would be best if he concentrated on his studies. Thirty-one years later Phillip Sharp received the Nobel Prize in Medicine.

During all those years, very few of my workdays were less than ten hours. What finally beat me down were the weekends. In high schools there is some type of activity—athletic events, concerts, plays, meetings—nearly every night. Administrators have to supervise. There were many Fridays when I would arrive at school at 7:00 a.m., put in a hard day, grab a carryout, eat it in my office, go to the big game and keep my eyes peeled for bleacher idiots. My favorite Fridays were those with a sock hop after the game. Sock hops are nothing more than mating rituals. You can recover from a sixteen-hour Friday on the weekends, but not if there's another big game on Saturday.

After scores of years supervising sock hops, resolving student-teacher and teacher-teacher adulterous affairs and parents with psychopathic tendencies, an aging body, mind and soul wear down.

During brief quiet times on Sunday afternoons or during fitful sleep, I began contemplating whether adjusting to retirement would be too stressful. Then I would hear a soft voice in the distance, "No, it won't."

I checked with the state teacher's retirement system and discovered the monthly payout would be sufficient until Social Security and Medicare kicked in. Vera intended to teach a few more years, and, if necessary, I could always get a job selling hair-restorer or, with training, become a Wal-Mart host. If you decide to retire early, it's advisable to adopt this policy: Keep spouse working. Promise you'll cook, clean and meet her at the door each day with a glass of wine.

My time had come, but perhaps none of this concerns you and how you will prepare for retirement. Maybe it does. Your stomach is an indicator. Have you noticed knots forming? Is burnout causing heartburn? Do you sleep standing up like a horse? If you love your job, stay with it. But listen to your stomach. If it growls, groans and rumbles, then you need not worry about going through the pangs of adjusting to retirement.

Many of my friends and associates are retired or soon will be. I have a few friends in their 80's, particularly professionals, who still get up each morning, put on a suit-and-tie and go to the office. They're happy. Others work part time in various places in order to supplement their income or have something to do. One works part-time bagging groceries and enjoys watching and meeting people. A former music teacher, who is also a tech guy works part-time at Radio Shack and enjoys his work. Other friends hesitate to retire indicating, they have to keep busy, and are not sure what they would do with the time.

I asked a former teacher friend, who retired shortly after I did, if he had difficulty adjusting to retirement. He replied, "I sure did, but you know,

I adjusted the next day." It can be that easy—if you light the fuse.

If you're not sure yet, wait. If you're ready to retire, follow my rules:

1. *Enjoy working while you can.*
2. *The retirement day will come sooner than you think.*
3. *During your retirement, it's not how many breaths you take, but how many times your breath is taken away. (Thanks to George Carlin)*

The day finally comes. When exiting the workplace parking lot after the last day of work, you immediately enter an adjustment zone. Adjusting is nothing new, because you've been trying to adjust to life's proceedings since the doctor whacked you. Remember your first dance, your first kiss when you didn't even know how to pucker and the first time you—you know, on a desolate, backcountry road under a full moon in the back seat of a 1940 Chevy?

Remember your marriage adjustment process? It's a process where pure love is intermingled with occasional spats, disagreements and conflicts. Most of ours have been about money, sex, personality disorders and the TV. She wants to watch drama. It can't get any more dramatic than when the Red Sox and Yankees are tied in the ninth. But there are areas where my wife and I agree. Take fried chicken; I insist on a breast, and she prefers thighs and legs.

Adjusting to marriage is an ongoing process. When you are adjusting to retirement and both of you are locked up in a house together 24/7, you may find that marriage is more difficult to adjust to than retirement. Your wife may even say to you, "Why don't you get another job?"

The birth of children is an adjustment when you have to transfer your entire existence to them. When my wife and I had a daughter, a son and then twin sons in four years four months, it was like adjusting to another planet. Try it; no, don't.

After working for 35-40 years, the energy supply tank begins running on reserve, your mind begins skipping, and your nerve endings shorten. Although work is worthy and good for one's soul, there is a point when the daily grind grinds the working appendages to nubs. You become like a child, who can't wait for Christmas.

Suddenly, bang, bingo, you're retired. They've had the parties, the cake and the speeches. It was all somewhat hurried, because the other employees had to get back to their cubicles. The boss spit out the accolades comparing you to Albert Sweitzer or Mother Theresa. You heard words like diligent, productive and loyal and something about your sick-day record. And then you wonder if those happy, gracious words were offered because you'll soon be out of their hair.

The retirement gift makes it final. Many big corporate CEOs receive retirement severance packages containing bundles of cash plus a yacht and a bay to anchor it in. The profits of a company may have tanked, but a CEO is loaded with what are called options meaning an option to sell a file drawer full of stocks worth more than North Dakota.

When a hard-working middle-class American employee retires, the only option is to accept or decline the Timex watch, which you don't need if you're no longer punching a clock. If you're lucky, you'll get an engraved one: "To Earl, thanks for breaking your back for Consolidated."

After all my years busting some of my organs, they gave me a coffee mug and a plaque. And they blamed my cohorts and me for leaving kids behind, because we took God out of the classroom. It wasn't that. One of the reasons kids were left behind was that during most of my career, money was so scarce we never had enough chalk.

After the retirement party, your fellow workers went back to their stations, and you, smiling like a moron, wished them well. Some of those former fellow employees had tried knifing you in the back those past few years, but you'll soon forget them the first time, you're fishing and they're not. The boss, although incompetent, was certainly better than the one before who was indicted.

You take the remnants of the cake, your personal files, photos of the family and the watch, plaque or coffee mug and put them in the trunk. After settling in the driver's seat, you take the parking permit from the rearview mirror and rip it to shreds. Then, drive slowly in order to take one last glimpse of the firm. When you hit the street, you've immediately entered an adjustment zone. You don't need a license and there are no one-way streets, stop signs or speed limits. You can drive right on into a new day and watch a beautiful sunrise the next morning for the first time in years.

When God placed Adam and Eve in the garden, which, from all indications, was intended to be a state of semi-retirement, He said, "Adjust to that which is forbidden." They couldn't do it, and, for a time, neither could I. It's like suddenly nothing is forbidden. You've been on death row and the pardon comes. The war is over and you're discharged. You're a virgin, and it's your wedding night. However, there's one major adjustment you need to make.

It's based on the fact you've spent practically all your life with other people telling you what to do. Most were less qualified than you and had half as much sense, but they were the ones calling the shots, giving the orders, driving you to thoughts of not turning the other cheek. Parents say no, teachers say do and the boss says when, where and how. The wife/husband and kids tell you what, but don't tell you what it costs.

All your life, you've been indoctrinated, regulated and regimented. Your direction was pre-determined. As the years wore on, it became habit, a kind of robotic reaction to regurgitate the year, month and day before. Routine provides a certain sense of security. Stay on schedule. When the alarm sounds, get up. When the bell rings, move. When alarms, bells and whistles cease ringing, you begin hearing other chimes. It's the angels in heaven softly singing sweet songs from the retirement wing.

A Monday in the middle of a school year is an odd time for a school administrator to retire, but that's the way it worked out. Twenty-one years earlier, I had replaced a principal in a high school of 2,700 students in the middle of a school year when he took another job. My replacement spent a week with me and was quite capable of assuming my responsibilities. I had wanted to work right on through the last day and fade out inauspiciously. Skip the party and any fanfare, or the "Praise to God" he's gone. One day I was trying to scale one mountain as I'd done for 33 years; five days later, I was on the way to a higher one.

To get to Mt Everest you fly from Louisville to Atlanta to Seattle to Tokyo to Bangkok to Katmandu and then to Lukla, Nepal, which has the world's most exciting airstrip. It is a dirt strip partially covered with grapefruit size boulders on an incline rising up the side of a mountain. Being in the air for 24 hours (31 hours total trip time) provides time to think. Up to that point, I had never given thought to much of anything except distractions.

Although I now write nearly every day, I'd never kept a journal before, but fortunately kept one during all my trips after retiring. The following is a part of what I recorded on the plane on November 2, 1991:

"Knowing I would not see my family or hear from them for the next 49 days left me with a bit of hesitancy at departing. Too late—I'm off."

I had wanted to work "normally" through to the end. The last day was typical to a point. Had a parent conference at 7:15 a.m. Suspended three freshmen at 8:00 for breaking out lights and had a causal hearing for an emotionally disturbed student at 9:00. I did a few odds and ends until lunch and then hid out to write thank you notes until school was over.

I had feelings of relief and regret. I somewhat regretted I had not done some things differently. However, I felt a sense of relief—greatly relieved that I did not have to continue dealing with problems and conflicts day after day, hour after hour. I'd had enough conflict.

I awakened at the regular time—5:40 a.m.—on the last day of work. I had that same anxious feeling in the pit of my stomach as I always had in preparing for a day's activities. I had the same subtle uneasiness—a reluctant anticipation of the routine and the unknown. The morning after my last day at work, I awakened at 5:30 without the loosely tied knot in the pit of my stomach.

Although some people get knots in their stomach at 36,000 feet, I didn't. My stomach felt great as I sat back nearly totally relaxed and gave the adjustment process my best effort. I felt marvelous floating along just above the clouds. I was in a dream-like trance as the sun delicately pulled its golden-layered cape from the cover of the clouds. Somewhere over the top of the globe, I eased into the magical presentation of a million soft, white and bright candle-tipped stars. It's not dark up there; you can see through the night and sense a mystical power nudging at the fringes of your soul. My transformation was complete before touchdown.

CHAPTER 4

DID YOU RUN ALL THE WAY?

❖ ❖ ❖

During retirement, your knees will probably go bad. Sorry, but after about 60 years of standing, walking and playing tag with your grandchildren, a knee will react unfavorably. You get it fixed and then your other knee is under such strain that its cartilage rips. These orthopedic procedures are preliminary to the insertion of stainless-steel hinges where your real knees once were.

My orthopedic surgeon handed me a red magic marker and told me to mark an X on my bad knee. This preliminary procedure was to prevent my surgeon from getting confused if he's having a bad day. Then he drilled three holes in my leg. Using a teensy video camera and several miniature tools, he removed the trash, fortunately from the knee marked with the X. I hobbled around for a month thinking my life and particularly my legs, as I had known them, were over. Maybe I could take up fishing from a boat, watch birds or become a television critic.

"Doctor, I suppose my running days are over."

"No, you won't hurt your knee. Run tomorrow if you can stand the pain."

Is he a quack? I hobbled around for weeks. The swelling and the soreness wouldn't go away. Running with a cane would be like riding in a car with only three wheels.

Three months after the operation on my 65th birthday, I put on the running shoes, apprehensively took the first stride and the pain was not what I'd imagined it would be. Three months after that first easy jog, I ran the New York Marathon. A couple of days after the marathon, I took the medal to my surgeon's office.

"Do you have an appointment?" the receptionist asked.

"No, I just wanted to tell the doctor something when he gets a break. It will only take a minute."

"Sorry, but he's busy. I can make an appointment for you."

"No, but will you give him a note?"

I scribbled, "Doctor, you operated on my knee six months ago. I wanted to tell you I ran the New York Marathon last Sunday. Thanks."

When I was about to open the door to my car, the surgeon came running out into the parking lot in his white smock holding the note.

"You did what! Did you run all the way?"

"Of course I ran all the way. How do you think I got this medal?"

I explained I wasn't there to boast, but wanted him to inform all his patients that the knife doesn't necessarily mean that one can't continue normal physical activities. With medical assistance, rehab, proper training, preparation, the luck factor and a heavy dose of determination, the body can perform wonders. He shook his head and said, "I thought I knew something about knees."

Seven years later, when I was 72, my surgeon did the same procedure to my other knee. Three months after that operation, I ran a 10k race, then a 10-miler and a half-marathon three weeks after that. The first operation was 14 years ago; I'm still pounding the road.

Running is not for everyone, and I certainly am not suggesting that those who can't or prefer not to, need try it. Walking, biking, swimming or working on appropriate exercise equipment are considered less stressful types of exercising, particularly on the knees. Most fitness authorities consider swimming one of the most beneficial exercises, because it causes little stress on the joints. To me, swimming across the English Channel or any channel is for English ducks, which have become bored of Shepherd's pie and want to try French cuisine.

Why would anyone want to run like an idiot through retirement? What's the hurry? There is no hurry, but you'll speed up the end of your retirement if you don't care for your body, which means pounding the road, one way or another. Retirement is the time to take it easy, isn't it? A body wears down after mining salt for 40 years. Why retire and drip sweat? It's a decision you'll have to make.

I'm convinced that exercising regularly and vigorously—running in my case– keeps me emotionally, mentally and physically alert and healthy. Remember, it's only a 3x30 deal—a minimum of three times per week for 30 minutes, a small price to pay for feeling great. When I don't run for a week or two, I become lethargic, stale and grouchy. I begin feeling tired, listless and often find myself napping on the couch, hoping rest will restore some of the vanished energy. It doesn't.

Medical research substantiates the benefits of vigorous exercise. Not only is exercise beneficial to the body, some of the latest research reveals it helps preserve one's mental powers and stimulates the brain when its matter begins getting moldy during the aging process. I get my exercise running the roads, not running around the house looking for my car keys.

Although physically active in sports all my life, I did not begin running until I was in my late 40's. My friend Roger and I played racquetball after work a couple times each week, and he kept encouraging me to run with him on other days. It didn't seem like it would be fun, but I finally agreed to try it. It isn't much fun. You get hot, sweaty, sore, exhausted and your feet develop red lumps where fluid accumulates, which you have to prick with a needle. I couldn't imagine running non-stop for six miles, but we built up to that distance and I did it. I was proud of my accomplishment, and began noticing the invigorating feeling after other gasping, slobbering, pounding, senseless runs.

Roger then encouraged me to run races. Why would I want to run a race? I'm not a horse or a Greyhound, but I entered a four-mile race, and broke out of the gate like Citation at the Kentucky Derby. A little man on my back kept whipping me, and I ran as hard as I possibly could, wobbling, weaving and nearly collapsing at the finish line. This was absolute stupidity. Dummy, you have to learn to pace yourself.

During the past 25 years, I've run countless races, including over 30 half-marathons and 3 marathons. Racing is an endurance activity providing a challenge and a goal. To enter a half-marathon three months hence prompts one to train properly and it's an incentive to push a bit harder. Apparently, my competitive nature causes me to think I might become a Tiger Woods of the old-folks racing circuit. But to maintain a healthy body, you can go out and jog or walk at a moderate pace four or five times per week without trying to break world records.

In most running races, walkers are invited to participate, and many do. Whether it's a 3-mile race or a half-marathon, walkers are out there pounding the road. What if you can't walk or run? The courageous wheelchair racers are just as dedicated. When you run a race through the hills—doubling the fun—you'll be running down a hill and hear from the rear, "Wheelchair, wheelchair coming!" You get to the side quickly, because those guys go by you like a rocket.

I've talked to many friends and acquaintances, encouraging them to begin a running or walking program. Usually, the response is, "I know I should and think I might." Some do, but most don't. I explain how to work up to longer distances. Run or walk around the block the first day, go around twice the next day and you'll be surprised what you'll be able to do in two months. A three-mile run or walk won't seem as strenuous or tiring as when you did the four-block run the fourth day.

"I did the three-block walk as you said, but got so sore it was tough to get out of bed." OK, tomorrow when you get out of bed, hit the road again and run the soreness out. Having suspected it all along, they stare at me like I'm nuts. I can't explain it, but when my muscles are sore for whatever reason, I can dress warmly, go out and run at an easy pace and most of the soreness disappears. After running a long race or marathon, I get soreness in my legs that is quite severe. The day after my first marathon, my legs were so sore it was a struggle to get into the car. The experts recommend that after running a half or full marathon, one should go out the next day and run an easy 3-4 miles to eliminate the lactic acid lingering in the legs. It works.

I've had back problems for 40 years, and at times, they've been quite severe. Twenty-seven years ago, I went to an arthritic specialist, and she said some of my lower vertebrae were scrunched together. That ends my running, doesn't it? "Oh, no," she said. "Running is one of the best things you can do to strengthen your back muscles, which takes the pressure off your spine." Keeping the leg muscles strong also takes the pressure off the knees. When my back acts up, if it's not too severe, I can hit the road, run easy while maintaining proper posture for a few miles and whatever was out of place usually goes back in. It may sound ridiculous, but it works.

Go out in that freezing weather, and you'll catch pneumonia. Maybe you've been driving down a desolate road in a warm car and up ahead a runner is running with a thin layer of icy snow on his toboggan. He's not crazy, or cold; he's warm inside. I don't know why, but there have been times when I felt a sniffling, blah-type bug coming on, and went out, worked up a sweat and killed the bug before it spread.

Is rest for what ails you a myth? I had a sudden attack on a nerve in my left leg a few months ago. Something had pinched it, and it throbbed and hurt like a Mogul had put it in a spiked torture device. The doctor put me in a large MRI canister and told me I had arthritis in both knees, my lower spine and left hip.

"Thanks a lot. I suppose that ends my running."

"No, run and do whatever you want to do." I do. That's the essence of retirement, isn't it? Are you going to spend the waning days searching for a doctor who will advise you to go buy a posture-fitting couch and lie on it? You can save the money and buy a posture-fitting coffin when the time comes.

My knees hurt somewhat when I run, but the pain usually lasts for about eight minutes until my joints and body are warm and loose; then my knees feel like new. When finished, I put ice packs on my knees for 25 minutes and my legs and knees feel great the remainder of the day.

I've tried a few projects encouraging a few friends and relatives to commit to running, walking or some other exercise program. The response I get is something like what comedian Fred Allen said, "I like long walks, especially when they are taken by people who annoy me." I'm beginning to understand why my wife frequently asks, "Why don't you go run for two hours?"

There are numerous studies pointing out those who walk, bike or use a treadmill regularly attain healthier numbers for body mass index, blood pressure, insulin and body fats called triglycerides. Regular exercise also helps produce "good' cholesterol. People in countries who regularly walk or bike to work, the store and church are considerably less obese than Americans, who drive one block to get a burger and large fries. A super-large diet cola takes some of the guilt away.

One friend suffered from stress, depression and obesity. Her doctor told her to work up to the point of walking five miles per day. What about some drugs? No drugs. Walk five miles per day. It worked. Another friend brought her kids to track practice everyday and watched.

"Why don't you run with them?" I asked.

"I couldn't do that."

"Come along with me tomorrow and we'll run real easy a couple of times around the track."

She did. "Tomorrow you run three or four times around the track, and then build it up each day."

A couple of months later, I saw her, smiling and all bubbly.

"I ran a 10k race last Saturday," she said.

"How'd you do?"

"Great!"

Inactive older folks' bones become soft and brittle. It's not surprising to get a phone call that an aged relative has fallen and broken a bone. During her later years, I kept on my mother's case to do some walking every day. "You're not going to tell me what to do, but I'll walk a little to please you." She did and maintained a fairly, healthy body to the end.

Some of those friends, who've become projects, agree and begin to walk, trot or move their bodies in some fashion. With good intentions, most eventually cross a finish line, but paying the price becomes too steep. It's too hot or too cold, their muscles ache, their feet are raw or their walking partner's babysitter quit. Push the baby in a stroller. No, it's either too hot or too cold for the baby. There are thousands of excuses, but the only acceptable one for a day or two is, "My dog ate my sneaker."

It's not too hot or too cold for me. Well, sometimes it is, but running in 20-degree temperatures is not so tough if you're dressed properly. The latest in lightweight Gore-Tex apparel keeps you warm and dry. You have to learn how to dress in all kinds of weather, but in hot weather, you can only take off so many layers. A 75-year-old man running naked through the neighborhood will run right into a road-block manned by a swat team. The American Medical Association warns that running in temperatures over 83 degrees is hazardous to your health. Sitting in an air-conditioned bar or the family den nibbling on the contents from a plastic bag for hours on end is hazardous to your health. If you sit in bars, do not request a diet-Coke and Bud-light mix thinking it will prevent flab. It will kill you. Sitting in a four-star restaurant for three hours is also hazardous to your health.

I once ran down the middle of Las Vegas when it was 114 degrees. I ran in running shorts, but it might have been more appropriate in the Vegas culture to run in a fig leaf. Why did I do it? I wanted to have a new and different experience, and when entering the city limits of Las Vegas, you're expected to get a little crazy.

Elite marathoners prefer running at temperatures around 40-degrees. The ideal running temperature for me is 50 degrees. I can wear shorts and a shirt made from what's called science-dry material, which allows perspiration to evaporate and heat to escape. But waiting 10 minutes for the start of a race in 40-degree temperatures in a thin shirt and shorts causes mounds of goose bumps. When I'm standing amidst a mass of shivering humanity waiting for the gun to go off, my blue body asks, "Why am I standing here?" The gun finally fires and I'm jostling for position with miles and miles to go. God said we'd suffer and he's right. Then a beautiful, young lady in form-fitting tights sprints past. As I catch a whiff of her perfume and follow her glistening ponytail freely flapping like a wind cone at an airport, I understand why I'm out there.

No, there is a deeper meaning. I'm out there contemplating a kind of existential spiritualism. Pursuing a challenging body-mind endeavor carries with it a spiritual aspect. The body is a precious gift. Training and using it to near capacity, and doing the same with one's mental powers, results in a harmonious balance and condition, which nourishes and sustains one's inner spirit.

If you've ever been to a big race—there's no real reason to go unless you have a loved one running with a heart murmur—you've seen strange phenomena. If it's 35 degrees, you'll see the young, tough, fast guys dressed in skimpy clothing I'd wear in 70-degree temperatures, but they'll also be wearing gloves. Without gloves, your hands get colder than any other part of the body. Bare legs at 40 degrees are no problem. In the larger races, you'll frequently see runners dressed as Uncle Sam, Superman, Mickey Mouse, Bat Man and Robin and a couple Elvis Presleys. In my community, in and around Louisville, Kentucky, we observe New Year's Day by running the 10-mile Hangover Classic. It's a continuation of party time. The streets are deserted at 9:00 a.m. on that day, and as the herd goes by, groggy people peek curiously from curtained windows at the festive runners going by. A few of the guys run in tuxedos and others in party hats. Is there a better way to begin a new year? Possibly, but charging full force into a new year has advantages over beginning it with an icepack on your head.

Exercising is a habit just like eating. I always eat an oatmeal-raisin Power bar two hours before every race. Running on a full stomach is like running with weights attached to your shoes. Doing much of anything on a stuffed stomach induces an hour-long coma.

Although I sin occasionally by rolling off the health-food wagon, I've developed some good eating habits, like avoiding salt, sugar and fats, all harmful to one's health. Shaking white crystals over food alters the natural taste. Salt makes food taste bitter and sugar fattens. Hands are made for handshakes, not shaking saltshakers. For breakfast, I usually eat cereal topped off with a banana, whole-wheat toast with a bit of honey or jam and two cups of eye-opener coffee. For lunch, it's usually turkey, tuna or sardines and limited portions of salad and fruit. Sardines—yuck—are loaded with omega 3. Dinner is brown, white and green—brown bread, brown rice, white meat and green stems or leafy things. A spice-flavored vinegar is my salad dressing and fat-free frozen yogurt or sherbet replaced my addiction to ice cream. Three bites of a delicious piece of cake or pie is enough. If I eat more, it's like syrup running through my veins. Gatorade won out over soda pop and white meat over red. Doctors say juice from red grapes in corked bottles clears the inner tubes, so I force it down. I've also heard dry martinis prevent malaria, so if I go to a jungle, I'll need to be immunized. But burgers layered with bacon and cheese with sauce dripping down your chin tastes so good. Life is short. Why starve eating only whole grains, whole leaves and whole tunas? What I eat and why I eat has become a habit. And feeling good is habit forming.

Are you ready to get started on your eternal-life-on-earth program yet? All that's required is diet and exercise. There is only one rule to follow: DIET and EXERCISE.

Man, I don't feel like going out there today for my run. There's a stiff, cold wind blowing and the water dripping from my eyes and the slobber from my mouth might freeze. It seems like the wind-god always focuses on blowing a strong wind directly into a runner's face. Run east and the wind is blowing from the east. Turn around and the wind-god decides to shift the wind from the west. But running against the wind provides a better workout. Retirement will last longer if you workout.

If I ran only when I felt like it, I'd never do it. And it doesn't get any easier as the years pile on. The most difficult part is putting on the stinky sneakers and taking the first stride. Once I'm out there, it's not so bad. Go easy the first mile, warm up and get loose, and then, hey, glad I'm out here. After a brisk run and a shower, I'm 20 years younger.

What doesn't work is, I'll run later this afternoon, if I feel like it. Setting and following a schedule works for me. When I decide to run five miles at

4:00 today and run seven miles on Saturday morning, I'll do it. It's like punching the work clock by 7:59 or be docked. Set a time and hit the road.

The atmosphere at the big races for runners and walkers is exciting. The mob gathers at an early hour, sometimes in near darkness, and warms up a bit to get loose. About ten minutes before the race, runners squeeze together behind the starting line. Music with a rapid beat is playing, the TV cameras running and helicopters flying overhead.

In years past, it would take several minutes to get to the starting line after the gun sounded. After the gun, it took me over six minutes to get to the starting line at the New York Marathon. If you're running competitively, it's not fair. Technology has solved that problem. Now every runner wears a plastic chip or plastic strip on a shoe or around an ankle. When each runner reaches the starting line, a mat with wires underneath electronically records your starting time. Cross the finish line and the computer wires record the exact time of your race, which for me is usually disappointing. I'm disgusted unless I break a personal record. In long races now, a runner's time is electronically checked and recorded at various points.

A few years ago, I ran a half-marathon race, went home, showered, hit the easy chair and logged on to "Chicago Marathon." My oldest son, Tim, was running that race. I was able to track him at various points during the race. I probably knew his official time before he did. The marvels of technology—

give me the running chip and the TV remote, and you can have the other stuff, like cell phones. I've seen people do all sorts of things using a cell phone, but only one talking while running a race. It's not an appropriate time for your wife to call about a problem with Junior.

With about a half mile to go during my first half-marathon many years ago, I heard wheezing, huffing and puffing behind me. A little, old, gray-haired lady blew right past me. No way was I going to be humiliated, so I gave it every ounce, calorie, and gut-straining fiber I had remaining. It wasn't enough. There will never be another grandmother smoke me, so I went into intense training for the next race.

During retirement, there is a tendency to slack off when pursuing well-intentioned activities. Aging promotes and induces slack, and if you're not cautious and persevering, the gap between the goal and the effort is soon miles wide. When one is involved in a particular endeavor, it's beneficial to set and strive for goals that require considerable effort to attain. Before retiring, I competed in the rat race, at times savagely, and the last thing I intended doing after was competing against rats and other animals, including humans. There I was, competing against little, old, gray-haired ladies. I was provoked and vowed, "That will never happen to me again." It did, but it will never happen to me again.

The runner's mantra is, "no pain, no gain." What a horrendous thought! You're telling me retirement should be painful. No, I'm telling you writing this book is painful. I want to go lie down on the couch this very instant, pick up a book, remove the bookmark and read a page or two until I collapse into a semi-conscious stupor. It's painful thinking up the next series of words that make sense. Think I'll go grab a bite to eat or walk out into the sunshine. Maybe that will revive me. No, you sit here and finish this paragraph. OK, OK. What's painful is not doing much of anything.

There are two ways to run a race. One can run leisurely and moderately, enjoy the camaraderie and the scenery and cross the finish line without medics catching you before you collapse. Or, you can run competitively and win money, medals, trophies, crowns and laurel wreathes. However, only the top few of several thousand win money and trophies. As do most ardent runners, I compete against myself. Younger runners, those under 75, talk about a PR—personal record. Technology has made competitive running more challenging and fun. The electronic strip around the ankle provides exact times of each individual's race. Races are organized in sex and age group formats. Run a race on Saturday morning, log onto the MoronMarathon.com Sunday afternoon and there I am: Terry Cummins placed 2,265 out of 11,785 runners, most of whom were 30 years younger. He was third of 21 male finishers in the over 70 age group. He finished ahead of all but one of the 18 little, old, gray-headed grandmothers over age 65. It was humiliating.

Male and female divisions are calculated by age groups, such as 30-34, 35-39, 60-64, etc. I'm in the 70 and over age group, and do quite well, because most of the guys in this group are dead. I've placed first in a few races and usually place in the top two or three in my age group. In the Kentucky Derby half-Marathon last year, I placed second of 26 runners over 70. I'm a fortunate and lucky guy.

How does one run all out for 13.1 miles, and then without stopping, turn around and run 13.1 miles back to where you started? Marathoners say it's all in your head. It's either a state of mind, or a mindless state. I've never been big on rationality, or reality for that matter. But the reality is that man crawled, walked and learned to run after antelopes before bicycles and taxis services.

God gave us legs, although he'd probably re-design the knee if He had it to do over. What are legs for other than to tour a city? You see more details and features of a city running through the streets as fast as you can than riding in a taxi. The Marine Corp Marathon is in Washington D.C. They sent a form inviting me to participate in their race. Oprah ran it a couple of years before and if she could do it, so could I. After signing the form at the bottom agreeing that the Marine Corp would not be responsible if I was wounded, captured or killed, I sent it back.

Training for a marathon is like giving birth to a baby each week for three months. This may not be an accurate comparison, but I've heard my wife talk about the gory details of the birthing process a thousand times. Think it's a picnic running circles in a waiting room?

Provided a runner has been running 15-20 miles each week and has formed a base, proper training for a marathon is a minimum three-month program. As each week goes by, a runner increases the mileage. For the average runner, who is not trying to break records, five or six days per week are devoted to training runs of six to ten miles for four or five days. The longest run is usually on a weekend.

The long runs become longer each successive week. If eight miles is the long run the first week, it increases to 10 miles the next week, 12 the next and so on up to 22 or 24 miles. Two or three weeks before the marathon, a runner tapers off with shorter runs to preserve energy.

Does it sound like fun? It is when you taper off and give birth only once a month. The last couple of weeks before the race provide time for the body to recover from the strenuous training. You can't run the race if you can't walk to the starting line. My first marathon went something like this.

Lining up with more than 18,000 other disturbed people, I anxiously and nervously awaited the tour of Washington D.C. (District of Confusion.) The skimpy-clad mass included our stiff-legged vice-president, Al Gore, whose two daughters had convinced him to run with them. He should have stayed back at the office and assisted President Clinton, who was having domestic-affair problems up to his crotch in Monicagate.

Thousands of family and friends packed the small area around the Marine Corp Memorial, a statue depicting the raising of our flag on Iwo Jima. The Marine band played inspiring tunes to march to as red and yellow balloons were released into an overcast sky. Weather forecasters had predicted a near perfect fall day for the event, but what do Washington experts know? A cold 48-degree drizzle began to fall. Marines, Boy Scouts and runners have to be prepared. Putting a garbage bag over my body all the way down to my knees was one of the most sensible things I've ever done.

When the howitzer sounded to start the race, the sea of flailing humanity, 18,000 skinny legs and Al Gore's 2 chubby ones, stampeded toward the Pentagon. That's where big brass race in limousines to go plan wars. We circled the Pentagon and ran back past the starting point. After eight miles, there was no turning back. We ran across Key Bridge and made a brief tour through Georgetown, then down Constitution Avenue past the White House. After running for hours, various odd thoughts race through one's tortured mind. Is the president looking out his window?

"Hey, Hillary, come look. There goes an old guy running by in a giant black condom."

The cold drizzle continued as I passed the half-way point near the Capitol. A lithe young lady, who blew past me and saw me wrapped in a clinging, wrinkled garbage bag, commented, "You look like a California raisin."

Thousands of cheering spectators lined the Mall searching for loved ones. Collapse at the Smithsonian and become an exhibit. Shoot past the Lincoln Memorial—dedicated to the proposition that all men are "created equal," but some will need therapy. Past the FDR Memorial with "nothing to fear, but fear itself" and dehydration. Eight miles to go and breeze past Jefferson's place where "all men are endowed…with certain inalienable rights" including the right to pursue muscle spasms. I was so caught up in history I forgot what I was doing.

I raced across the Potomac and around the Pentagon again with two miles to go, then one. I can do it! Charged up, I sprinted and ripped the garbage bag off so my number would show at the finish line. Finally, I charged up the steep hill to the Iwo Jima Memorial and a Marine Corp officer placed a medal around my neck and said, "Congratulations, sir." Wearily staggering through the mud, I shed a joyous tear or two and gave thanks.

I creamed Al Gore, beating him by 57 minutes. George W. Bush eked by him by the skin of about 500 hanging chads. I placed 23rd in the 123 males in the 60-64 age group. After my accomplishment, I thought about going into politics. No, it would be like running a marathon every day and then lying about it. What do I do next? Why not tour New York City by rapidly moving one foot in front of the other?

One year later, after training senselessly, I decided to take a day off, relax and play golf with dear friends. One dear friend was a like a wild man swinging a club. He hit me with a line-drive bullet in the—how do I put this? He hit me in the area where a male uses a specific object to fertilize a female egg. My doctor, who was also the doctor of my dear friend, who had maimed me, suggested I sue him for $4 million if I was unable to sire children again.

New York was postponed for a year. When the infamous day finally arrived a year later, 31,000 dummies with a one-way ticket rode buses to the starting gate on Staten Island. To reach the Promised Land runners had to sprint across the Verrazano-Narrows Bridge, cut through Brooklyn, Queens, the Bronx and Harlem before entering the pearly gates at Central Park in Manhattan. All was going quite well after 16 miles, but when I was sprinting (lumbering) across the Queensborough Bridge, a mugger or somebody caused one of my calf muscles to go into a spastic fit. I nearly went down, but, fortunately, a medic appeared out of nowhere and led me off the bridge to a medical aid station.

"Get on the cot," the medic ordered. I fell on the cot hoping she'd remove the red-hot poker from my leg. She pounced on me like a big cat, took her blacksmith-like paws and dug them deeply into my exploding calf muscle. If the Empire State Building had been adjacent, I would have gone through the tent roof and rocketed up to at least the 40th floor. She continued clawing and digging until I would have gladly signed permission to amputate. After several minutes of this torture—next time water-board me—she handed me a cup of water, an energy gel pack and said, "Hit the road." It was one of the funniest things I've ever heard in my life. Ten miles to go, I'm crippled and she says, "Hit the road," She helped me stand up and I wobbled out onto First Avenue, where people lined the street cheering. Were they cheering for me? I can't let them down. Not having money for a taxi and not wanting to taste bitter defeat and humiliation, I raised my bad leg and pushed off with the good one. Not too bad, although most of my remaining strength was on the cot back in the emergency tent.

It went fairly well, except about every mile or so I'd feel another muscle spasm coming on. Forced to stop, I'd say a bad word, dig it out with my fingers like she did and move on.

Is there a better way to tour the Big Apple than strolling through Central Park on a beautiful autumn day? With about a quarter mile to go up a hill, of all things my leg cramped again. I dug at the spasm like a gravedigger as other weary runners passed me gleefully. Glee is evasive until 100 feet from the finish. Finally, I stumbled across the line with a time of 4:48. I finished 22,265 out of 31,785 runners and placed 88th of 261 runners in the 65-69 age group. Disappointing, but considering the 20 to 30 minutes I lost fighting off the sudden lumps forming in my legs, I couldn't be too distraught. There is a physical and mental power and another sustaining one. Whatever that source may be, I'm eternally grateful.

I'd never before developed cramps when running. Research later revealed consuming too much water and other liquids the day and hours before a long run induces cramping. I'd spent the previous day guzzling water like crazy to insure hydration, but apparently overdid it.

I awakened early the next morning knowing I needed to walk around the city to work out the kinks and soreness. One of my sons and I arrived at the World Trade Center when it opened. From the top, we watched the city come alive that early Monday morning. I could see Staten Island, the Verannazo-Narrows Bridge and much of the route I'd run the day before. The city was so full of life the day before. However, it was a new day, and a wonderful day in my life.

Less than two years later, man took the towers down. Our lives can be ground into despair's rubble, or we can rise again to greater heights. This principle applies to both young and old.

I've always wanted to love Paris in the springtime. After a sleepless night on a modern 737 (737 is the number of times they search you for weapons), I arrived in beautiful Paris, France in April 2002 to run the Paris Marathon. After checking into the Napoleon Hotel adjacent to the Arc de Triumphe, I met the other members of our marathon team, who had also made a commitment to run for the Aubrey Fund for Pediatric Cancer Research at the Sloan-Kettering Cancer Center in New York. Aubrey, who accompanied us, was diagnosed with cancer at age four and had a 10 percent chance of living. She won the battle, began running in her teen years, and then established the means for others to compete for a worthy cause and contribute to pediatric cancer research. Most of our 18-team members ran in honor of a friend or family member who was battling cancer. Through continuing research, children with cancer now have a 55 percent chance of conquering the disease and resuming a normal life. Our team raised over $65,000 to assist in the battle.

As part of the agreement and commitment, the plane fare and four nights in the wonderful Hotel Napoleon were provided. In addition, team members received shirts, caps, a running uniform, a pre-race evening meal, a post-race meal and party, food and massages after the run and other incidentals. In addition, spouses (Vera accompanied me) or a friend could stay with us in the hotel rooms at no cost. Paine-Weber, to whom I am very grateful, contributed all these extras.

It was springtime in Paris, and romance seized the fragrant air. Blossoms were appearing along the Champs-Elysees. The hotel was elegant; the cuisine superb. The Eiffel Tower majestically pointed towards the clear blue sky, and in the Louvre, Mona Lisa was smiling more than ever. There was only one problem. I had to go run a stupid marathon.

With one full day to recover from jet lag and the apprehension and excitement, I finally fell asleep at about 4:00 a.m. on the night before the race. Three hours later, I staggered to the starting line a block from my hotel at the Arc de Triomphe and nervously joined the other 30,000 runners on the cobblestones of the Champs Elysees. With flags and balloons waving, music blaring, instructions in French, which meant absolutely nothing to me, and sand grinding away at my sleepless eyes, I realized there was no turning back. After several months of intensive training, why go through all the effort and then surrender to the French?

The course led us down the Champs where the French sat at morning coffee, staring quizzically at the thundering herd. After charging around Place de la Concorde, we had only 25 more miles to go. I confidently forged on, past elegant buildings that make Paris one of the most beautiful cites in the world. Sprint to the River Seine, past the Notre Dame Cathedral and then sprint toward the Eiffel Tower. What other alternative is there when you're in a no-stop zone? Through another park and then I spotted the Arc de Triomphe and the finish line with thousands of spectators greeting and cheering us. My emotions must have been like those of Charles de Gaulle when he gave the victory speech at the end of World War II. It was a war, but my 4-hour, 25-minute excursion through Paris saved me over 50 tour-bus Euros, and the experience was incredible.

How often do I hear, "Running at your age, or any age, will eventually maim, cripple or kill you?" Eventually, something will. If I have a choice, I'd rather reap my eternal reward struggling to cross a finish line than stuck in an old-folks home.

CHAPTER 5

HOW TO KEEP YOUR MIND DURING RETIREMENT

❖ ❖ ❖

Life has a beginning, a long middle and a brief pause, commonly known as retirement, before the end. Most of us try avoiding the end, because the unknown is uncertain. There are four phases in this cycle: growing up, grown up, tapering off and the final rest-in-peace phase, which implies what prior rest we had was usually interrupted.

Growing up is painful. Remember when your first love ditched you, when your heart was ripped apart? Then during the long grown-up phase, you struggled and worked to feed and clothe your children and the ordeal of having their teeth braced. When the last child flew the nest to who knows where, we then began to count the days.

A friend once told me he had one year, 239 days and, looking at his watch, three hours to go before retirement. Was it because he had a get-me-out-of-here job? Perhaps counting the days to retirement is understandable. It doesn't make sense, nor will it preserve what sense we have to retire and begin counting the days until finality, whether it is a return to dust or eternal rest.

Retirement is another fork in the road. Thought I was finished trying to find my way. Nope, one fork leads to retiring (Webster says, "withdrawal from action."), but living each retired day filling in blank spaces gets tiring. The other fork leads to "re-tiring." Say you dug ditches for a living, which is very tiring whether you were using a bulldozer or a shovel. Ardently pursuing an activity like digging holes to plant roses and hoeing a beautiful garden is re-tiring, and it can refreshingly spark a reserve energy and vitality we didn't know we had.

Unfortunately, as the years pass by, so does the body and mind. Normally, this bypass is not swooped away as when a bolt of lightening strikes, but is a gradual grinding away of our physical prowess and mental faculties. When the body begins to go, what good is it to have your mind focused on gallstones followed by dizzy spells followed by an irregular heartbeat? And presuming there was one originally, how can the mind retain its sharpness when the primary stimulation is from the boob tube?

It's all the more reason to rage against the pre-permanent rest phase in order to postpone the fourth and final one. When you retire from the work force, you'll need dark clothing appropriate for funeral home visits. Your peers will often be resting there, and you'll be expected to make fitting comments. "He's gone to a better place," is always encouraging, but it doesn't say much for the place he was in. Do not say, "We'll miss him," unless you really mean it. And it's not advisable to say, "He looks so natural." Although death is natural, no one looks natural when it happens.

Tired of hearing use-it-or-you'll-lose-it? However, your body is as important to you as your car. You dread a treadmill? So do I, but not as much as I dread hearing, "He's gone to a better place." I like the place I'm in, and when I get to the better place, running on streets paved with gold is a sure cure for arthritis.

Before addressing ways to keep your mind, another aspect or component to consider is your spirit. The spirit is difficult to pin down, because it tends to be elusive. When we are aware of its presence, it might go poof, leaving us alone, lonely and with feelings of despair. Now this is where it gets tough trying to define the spirit and the soul. I once attempted to write an article defining the soul. A scholarly theologian would have burned it at a stake. How do you define something that may or may not exist? It seems to be a you have it or you don't proposition. I feel nothing, or I feel something always hovering around me, fleeing and then returning to remain with me.

In part, our mind and heart decide which journeys we take. Maybe a soul is something like the heart and mind joined together, guided by a rambling kind of spirit. To avoid winter snows, we can fly to where it doesn't blow. But frequent-flyer miles are unnecessary for a spiritual flight, an exploratory journey expanding beyond this earthly realm.

A clearer definition would be helpful—or better yet, paint a picture. Michelangelo's depiction of God reaching out to give man life and a soul is about the best one we have. Through the ages, philosophers and theologians have tried explaining and clarifying aspects of the nature of the soul, but it remains questionable, arguable and, "Are you kidding me?" Blaise Pascal, a 17th century French theologian, tossed it back in our laps. "There are some statements that cannot be fathomed; God exists or he does not exist; the soul exists in the body or we do not have a soul; the world was created or it was not created."

So, take it from there. It's been said that if you question the existence of God, go jump in a foxhole with bullets whizzing over your head. If you believe there is a supreme spiritual component to life, accompanied by a soul, shouldn't it be given attention and nourished?

If you believe a soul exists, when the numbers of your days begin diminishing, it might be advantageous to settle down a bit and interact with the force which placed us here for the purpose of illuminating each day.

As our younger and productive years decline and the sun dips closer to the horizon, isn't it advisable to have an insurance policy with an eternity clause? Knock on the gate, and the judge will want to see your resume'.

The truth is, our guideline for admission to eternity is that when you quit your job on earth, you get a little breather, but you should keep you life's bucket near the brim. You have a part in the continuation of our Big Bang process. Expansion applies to you as it does to the glow of another star, except a star doesn't have a choice. What is creation all about, if not your contribution to the process?

Retirement provides time. Mathematically, there are eight to ten more hours per day available to meditate, think and contemplate. More time to study, consider and reason, more time to wonder, imagine and create.

There's time to take longer walks in a woods and time to sit by a sea. There's time to romp and play with our grandchildren, but don't overdo it, or you'll be staring at a wall with an icepack on your thigh.

During our advanced and advancing years, there is more time to ponder the unfathomable mysteries of life, quieter moments to celebrate creation's parade and time to enrich the soul. Need convincing? Hold a little child, who is in deep and peaceful sleep. Each breath you hear renews the faith, and both hearts seem to beat as one.

After writing the last word of my first book six years ago, I rolled my chair back greatly relieved. Then something touched me. I think it was my soul. Whatever the merits of the long, hard journey, it was my creation, fueled and sustained by an accompanying spirit prompting and guiding me.

A number of years ago, I heard Jesse Stuart, a well-known Kentucky author, ask his audience, "How many of you have to write?" I do now. Call it a passion, compulsion or obsession, I must write, but it's tough. One writer described writing as sitting down with a blank piece of paper and opening a vein. Another explained that the words appear after beads of sweat begin dripping from the brow. Thornton Wilder quipped, "An incinerator is a writer's best friend."

Learning to write is like breaking a leg and then learning to put one foot past the other. Begin with crutches and then a cane until you can walk. Then hit a stride and keep running all the way. At first, it's painful, but keep moving until the kinks disappear. Writing is putting one word, sentence, paragraph and page after the other. Writing begins on crutches, and after years of hobbling along wadding up pieces of paper and tossing them, a writer hopes to find a reader, who responds with a gleam in his eye.

Writing a weekly column and this book, with another in the works, at my age is like retiring and then marrying a beautiful, young fertile woman, who yearns for a brood of children. Writing a book is a nursery full. It's a room full of little chapters rolling around, scattering in all directions. I gently gather them up and try putting some sense into their heads.

Why must I write? It feels as if it is a vital part of my existence. Why does anything exist at all is the eternal question. What is existence? We understand chickens exist to cross the road. Which existed first, the chicken or the egg? What makes the difference? If a chicken wants to risk its neck crossing the road, let it. Adventurous humans do it all the time. We do not know the range of a chicken's IQ. Apparently, some are smart enough to observe friends getting smashed, and perhaps that's why the older, experienced ones don't run to the other side.

In the previous "run all the way" chapter, the why, how and importance of keeping the body fit was stressed. General Douglas McArthur said, "Aging wrinkles the body, quitting wrinkles the soul." No matter the age, an unused mind withers and flounders on what is often considered as the safer side.

There are scads of material available on how to keep one's mind. Some of the latest studies reveal physical exercise stimulates brain function. One keeping-your-smarts expert recommends getting down on the floor and doing exercises to stimulate blood flow to your brain. Then you have to pump blood back into your legs to get back up. Other young experts on aging recommend everything from working puzzles to learning a new language. I thought about learning a new language because English keeps changing. Encyclopedia is now Wikipedia and a photo album is Facebook. Twitter is a postcard and a text is not a book. We should do whatever it takes to prevent, "Seen my keys?" and "What's his name?" Oh, for the good old days when the memory button wasn't turned off.

The best way to keep your mind during retirement is to use it, whatever the level of the gauge on your cognitive tank. Not that mine is half-full, but writing keeps my clog-prone cogs turning. Staring at a blank piece of paper or a new Word document until the sweat drips is like hitting the "wall" at 20 miles in a 26.2-mile marathon. The body slows to a crawl and the mind spits and sputters like a car with dregs in the tank. Since we can't be traded in, the only remedy is a daily tune-up.

Although I served in the military and diligently slaved for my family for more years than I can remember (there are advantages to dementia), I am undisciplined. As I write this, tomorrow is a new year. Tomorrow morning I must run the Hangover Classic, a ten-mile race through the streets of downtown Louisville, Kentucky. The temperature will be in the lower 20's when we start. Hope it's no more than in the mid-20's when I finish, which is better than staggering out of bed hung over.

When the alarm clock is finally tossed into a compactor, we are then unscheduled, and there is that tendency to settle on Easier Street. Retirement requires self-discipline, or else you'll become a blob with zombie-like characteristics. Who else will do for you what you need done, the government? In the military, you learn to march lockstep, and if you don't, you're dirt. But retirement is doing what you want to do, isn't it? It is, but if you are going to do it as best you can, or better than you ever thought you could, shape up, fall in line and, "Company A, forward march." If you stay in place, they'll capture you.

Whatever the reason, I've had the urge and desire to write since my college days, and intended to pursue it someday when I had the time. I'm not sure why or how it happened.

My elementary education at the four-room Goforth School provided the basics to go forth to high school or back to plowing. After eight grades, I advanced to Morgan High School so I could play basketball in a real gym with a roof and continue my education on the side. Our library was composed of books stacked on four shelves at the back wall of a classroom, and our science experiments were limited to memorizing words like protozoa and paramecium. I took four classes each day, practiced basketball during fifth period, and went back home to plow, milk and feed the livestock until dark. Farm boys and girls have work to do and little time for books.

I learned how to hit a basket with consistency, graduated from high school and moved on to a much higher level. I soon discovered Transylvania College was considerably higher than I'd anticipated. They had teachers who held doctorates in their heads. I hadn't realized how smart a person could be. It took tons of learning to fill in the wide gap between us.

They said I needed English, which I'd already studied for 12 years. The problem was I had to read what they called classics and then write about why it was a classic. What can you say about Wordsworth, who said he wandered lonely as a cloud, or explain why a Greek had an Oedipus complex? It was tough.

When you cut and harvest tobacco under a sweltering August sun, it's tough, too, but you keep at it. So I handed in papers, and they handed them back with comments essentially meaning, "You don't know how to cut tobacco, do you?"

My English classes were fascinating. With miles to go, why did Robert Frost stop to watch a woods fill up with downy flakes? Shakespeare could have you laughing on one page and then make you feel like you'd been stabbed on the next. I sweated it out and kept on moving down the composition row. However, my words would be reversed, my sentences fragmented and my commas dangled in the wrong places, which classified me as bordering on being half-literate. Occasionally, I'd get back a paper with a red arrow pointing to a sentence, with something like, "Insightful and well stated." And I recall one solemn professor who read my paper to the class and laughed out loud, because he liked it and thought it amusing. There were those few slight rays of hope, a glimmer that maybe someday I could learn to write.

After receiving a degree signifying a degree of intellectuality, I went into the Navy to help protect free speech, got out and worked like a famished dog for years. Initially, when I retired, I wanted to enjoy freedom from bondage for a while, and do some things I had longed to do. I'd try writing after some fun and travel and after episodes of extreme laughter watching workers stalled in early-morning rush-hour traffic.

It's too easy to fall into a put-it-off trap after you get a gold watch or an inscribed coffee mug. You can easily be diverted to three-hour lunches or a seashore or spend an exorbitant amount of time looking for the best deal on tires, house paint and chicken breasts. But beware of an evil spirit, who will tempt you to refrain from exerting both body and mind. This satanic force, specializing in self-destruction, wants you to perish.

Although I knew I would someday write the story of my grandfather who raised me, it took 12 years from the time I officially retired until I completed and published the book. Why so long? It was simply because I was undisciplined and distracted by sinful things like golf, followed by reclining positions in preparation for happy hour followed by drowsiness and a stupor.

My retired friends kept asking me to join them on golf courses and during these weak moments, I'd go hit at a ball until I made contact. Then I would go to a knee-high rough or thick forest and look for the ball. It made no sense, as is late life without purpose. I also became an on-call Mr. Fix-It person in my own home. Dull paint and clogged drains never end. Why fertilize the lawn and then sharpen the mower blades to cut the growth? A male retiree has to be careful not to become a jack of several trades. There were many times I'd have a monkey wrench in my hand and question why I was not holding a pen over paper instead.

One other note of caution; do not retire so you can spend more time with your family. If your spouse is working, encourage him/her to continue and promise to cook dinner, do the dishes and remove the dust occasionally. If your middle-aged, immature children have children and live close by, move. No, but you'll need to budget gasoline if you're going to provide a family Gray Cab service. If you think work was boring, sit on a soccer field three late afternoons per week. It's torture until little Tim tries and tries to kick a ball but misses. It will break your heart. Another pertinent point, when growing up; I didn't practice anything. You don't practice milking cows; you milk them. I milked them, two spigots at a time with both hands pumping vigorously.

Soon after I retired, my daughter and her husband, who both worked at other jobs, decided to raise buffalo on their beautiful farm about 20 miles away. Oh, great; I knew how to farm and could help them. I'd grow the food in the garden and herd buffalo like the cattle we had back on the farm. Buffalo, like people, are reluctant to be penned in a corral. Writing was delayed until the buffalo roamed at a new range.

There are two ways to write words on paper, type or use a pen. I'd never learned to type and gradually my hand developed a condition whereby I couldn't control a pen.

Therefore, technology was forced on me. I avoid high tech, because it's de-humanizing. When friends totally ignore me because either they are on a cell phone or squinting and punching an iPod, I talk to myself, or a dog, which is man's best friend.

Morgan High School was located on the South Licking River. It was too tempting to gaze out the window wishing I was fishing, but we had learning to do. Farmers don't need typing, but girls do so they can become secretaries for high school principals. While the girls learned typing, boys studied agriculture and learned better ways to castrate boars, rams and bulls, which I already knew. Well, maybe not a better way. But how many retirees do you know who run a castration service?

When I put a pen to paper, my hand shakes like a wet dog. It looks like Sanskrit. During retirement, you'll find that your outer extremities can become uncooperative. Unfortunately, it may work inward toward your vital center, at which time you should have more tests run or be content watching television.

My daughter writes my checks and completes other forms for me. When I have to sign my name, I'm embarrassed. The specialists tested everything including the nerves in my arms to the waves in my brain, which was a bit alarming. What if your waves were waving in the wrong direction or jumping and skipping? They couldn't determine the cause of my loss of control—hand not head—and sent me to a rehab center. The nice, young finger specialist had me practice writing the alphabet between wide lines like kindergarten children do.

"If you put a gold star on this, can I take it home and tape it to our refrigerator?"

On an old floppy disk computer, I taught myself to search, pick and peck. Then I had to figure out how to move the arrow up to "new word document" and click. There it was, a blank piece of paper inside a screen. Sweating, I mastered the mechanics of being physically able to record a word following another. Now, all I had to do was jump into an incinerator and open a vein. Drops of blood began dripping down on the keypad.

Finally, I forced myself back to a schedule and a routine, similar to having a real job. On most mornings, I'd get dressed, drive the few miles to the library at Indiana University Southeast, a branch of Indiana University, plug in my laptop and write. I sent out articles to newspapers and syndicates, and waited to select the one which paid the most, but newspapers avoid stuff that warrants shredding.

I'd go home at night and read Ellen Goodman, Dave Barry, George Will and many other talented columnists who are the masters. Up the next morning, back on the job and writing another article, better than the last one, maybe. Toss it and then another. When I stumbled on a word too "big" for me, I'd write it down, look it up and keep a long list, an attempt to refute the presumption that an old dog can't learn new words.

I don't have a clue why, but I write when I'm running, eating, watching TV and driving. The nights I try to fall asleep and can't is because I'm writing. I'll be running along a road gasping for air when something in the air tells me to change a sentence or a word in the third paragraph of the article I'm writing, or I'll be driving in thick traffic thinking of a topic for my next column. It's dangerous for the mind to wander; you could crash into a driver concentrating on his cell phone conversation with his perturbed wife. I can't stop writing, can't stop trying to transfer thoughts, ideas, opinions, descriptions into a body of words better than the previous one. A few days ago, I was out running and began designing the back cover of my book, not this one, but the next one.

OK, my mind is messed up, but not completely. I could be working on my putting or digging dandelion roots from my lawn. The mind of an aging person can be like a blooming rose or like a dandelion absorbing insecticide.

Pick an interest you had thoughts about trying someday and pursue it. I have a retired friend who makes jewelry and other types of decorative boxes. Another friend loves his garden and experiments with developing new varieties of day lilies. Another roams hills and valleys photographing wild flowers. Create something. You have the time, so do it before time runs out. If creation stops, so do you.

When I was a principal, a father who had little formal education stopped by my office to discuss the subjects his son should take. I suggested Algebra II. He explained that since his son was interested in following in his father's footsteps on the farm, he wasn't sure Algebra II would be of benefit. I explained that more advanced subjects would be challenging, and, who knows, Elmo Jr. might want to continue his education beyond high school someday. "You're right," he said, "If nothing else, it would tantalize his brain."

When that tantalizing, stimulating force begins taking longer rests as we age, waking up is harder to do.

The first sentence of the first article I published was, "Modern man faces two dreadful obligations—paying taxes and taking his grandchildren to Disney World." The article was published in the magazine section of the Louisville Courier-Journal, as were a few others until the magazine was discontinued. I kept writing articles and sending them to other papers. Most responses were similar to one postcard I received with two measly words, "No thanks."

Eventually, two Indiana newspapers, the New Albany Tribune and Jeffersonville Evening News, both CNHI newspapers, began publishing my weekly articles at the ripened age of 66. Wouldn't you think that after more than 500 articles in print, I would never end a sentence with a preposition?

Taking your grandchildren to Disney World is fun, if you can stand it. I primarily write humor, irony and political satire. I write the truth, or 98 percent of it is. My readers can determine the two percent that is stretched a bit. Political satire is perhaps my favorite genre, because the material is abundant and politicians do outrageous things. It couldn't, didn't happen, but Bill Clinton stained Monica's blue dress in the Oval Office of all places. George W. Bush stood on an aircraft carrier holding a pilot's helmet under a banner declaring, "Mission Accomplished." Add Hillary, John McCain, Sarah Palin and Dick Cheney, who shot a guy in the face, and the material is overwhelming.

George Barnard Shaw said his way of joking was telling the truth. There is no way to tell the truth about the role of the blue dress in the impeachment proceedings without sidesplitting laughter. Writing satire requires imagining all sorts of scenarios. I've written several articles about imagined conversations of the first couple in bed at the White House. Imagine Laura consoling George when he sees a bin Laden ghost during a nightmare, or Michelle on Barack's case about his lack of experience bailing out the banking and automotive industries.

"Everything in nature is lyrical in its ideal, tragic in it destiny, and comic in its essence," according to George Santayana. A writer has a choice between writing about the mournful and tragic, or the amusing and comic. I prefer the essence, which is invariably comic and absurd. Politics is absurd, as is family. The unpredictable and complex behavior of individuals often borders on the epitome of absurdity and stupidity. Just take a brief glance at your immediate environment.

I'm often asked where, why and how I pick my topics. Read the newspapers, watch the news and observe the human condition as it flounders. Observation and imagination are my primary tools. The imagination has few bounds. I turn it loose and let it run wild and free. When it returns—bingo—the idea sticks and words begin to appear.

Employees at a corporation protested when management ran a save-toilet-paper campaign. The history of toilet paper is fascinating. Why does the female bladder fill so quickly after driving four miles in a car when the husband is in a hurry? With my 10-year-old grandson riding along, I drove up to an ATM, punched the pin number and 100 bucks slid out. My grandson asked, "How do you get money out of a bank when you don't work?" It was an opportunity to write about how Social Security provides social insecurity. Before this past Christmas, I peered out my window. About 100 robins were attacking my tall holly tree. They ate every red berry and then flew the short distance to the tree over my car, depositing purplish, gooey, sticky seeds all over it. My article explained that, although I'm an above average holly hanger, this year, our holiday décor would be primarily plastic.

I write about my grandchildren, family vacations, and marriage and its conflicts, like when both husband and wife collide at the kitchen sink, or meet on a staircase when one is going up and the other down. What is funnier than marriage and family? I write about arthritis, cataracts, torn cartilage and the woes of aging. When and if you regain consciousness, various aspects of surgical procedures are humorous. I write about Google, Tweet and cell phoning, the current plague. Human relations have been reduced to a cell phone implanted in one ear and the other gone stone deaf.

Compare that to my growing up on the farm without electricity. Eventually, when our house was wired, the kerosene lamp was history. Miraculously, when I pulled a string, a faint light glowed from the ceiling. Sixty years later, my wireless laptop is susceptible to becoming infected with a virus, deleting all my hard-earned work inside my hard drive. Life was simpler in a hayfield.

There are ways to save our work and ways to save the memories of days gone by. The modern way is OK up to a point, but the old ways provided much more time to sit on the front porch swing watching the moon come up and the fireflies do their dances. Too bad the sleeping pill has replaced the front-porch swing, which settled our nerves for a good night's sleep.

How Did Back Then Become Right Now? is a collection of 71 of my articles. Most of them make some reference or comparison to how life was back in the old days. Who cares? Older people remember those days and relate to them, but the young think milk is squeezed from milkweed like orange juice from a tree. The vast difference between now and back then is incomprehensible to the younger generation. Hi-tech for us was a hand cranked butter churn.

One of my articles explained how we harvested hay in the old days using a pitchfork and muscular arms. We mowed it with a mowing machine pulled by horses. We then forked it eight times by hand. The process included stacking, loading, unloading and pitching it in a hayloft. Each winter day the hay was pitched down from the loft into a pile. Then, using a fork, the hay was distributed to the animals in the barn. After they devoured and digested it, the waste was loaded on a wheelbarrow, wheeled to the manure pile and dumped. In the spring, we'd wade into the mountainous manure pile, fork it to a wagon and finally to a field where it was unloaded and spread over the land. The nutrients supplied nourishment for another bountiful crop and another year working in harmony with nature's wonders.

Today, a farmer climbs into the air-conditioned cab of his powerful tractor, turns on the stereo and using mowers, rakes, balers, forklifts and other mechanized equipment "pitches" his hay with a hydraulic lift. It can be monotonous and tiring cramped up in a soft seat turning a steering wheel from sunup to sundown.

The difference between now and then is like night and day. What I remember about back then was the ample daylight. Modern days are not perpetually dark, but covered with a haze. From then to now, the pitchfork has been replaced by the forklift and the fireplace by the thermostat. The fireplace in our kitchen was about five feet wide. In winter, I'd hurry each early morning from the frost-covered featherbed to the warm flickering flames. Standing by the roaring fire was a moment to dream about easier times. Mark Twain and Robert Frost didn't adjust a thermostat. Abe Lincoln didn't open a new Word document to record his address at Gettysburg. Some of the best thoughts ever written were penned on scrap paper as Lincoln did on the back of an envelope. Sofia Tolstoy, Leo's wife, hand copied and re-copied *War and Peace* and all his other books between giving birth to their 13 children. Write a book now, and simply e-mail it to the publisher. It saves postage.

The seed for the book I would write someday was planted many years before. Growing up and being raised by my grandfather on a hill farm in Kentucky was a story embedded in my soul, where it remains. I had the title for the book 34 years before writing it. On my first trip abroad in 1968, I attended a Sunday service in Westminster Abbey in London. Compared to where I received God's word at the Short Creek Baptist Church perched on the highest hill in Pendleton County, Kentucky, poet's corner where I sat in Westminster Abbey was overwhelming. The only similarity of the two churches was both ministers used the same source for their messages. The minister at Westminster took his inspiring message from John 21:17. Peter asked Jesus three times how he could love him more. Jesus replied, "Feed my sheep," When I left the historic abbey, the voice was clear. I had the title for my book—*Feed My Sheep.*

After I left the farm for college and the years went by, I knew someday I would return, reliving the times when my grandfather taught me how to feed our sheep, how to work, dream, live the good life and become a man. How would I write the book? What approach would I take? We can't recapture the past by going home again. Yes, we can if our spirit wills.

My spirit, fleeting at times, nagged for many long years until I finally sat down and wrote the first paragraph. What took me so long? (What is taking you so long?) It was this and that. There was no explanation, other than there were too many reasons and excuses to prolong taking the plunge. Who wants to retire and then "re-tire?" If working is tiring, write a book. It's like opening every vein in your body. Surprisingly, a timely transfusion boils your blood again, turning on the heat.

I'm unaware how professional and reputable writers write about times past, but I went back and lived what I wrote. At age 69, I reverted to age 13. The transformation was a giant step back in time, but I was there amidst the sweet aroma of the fresh mown hay and apple blossoms in spring. I entered the musty barn where the animal scents were distinct and strong, but refreshingly cleansed by nature's means. I could smell the hams and bacon sides curing beside sacks of sausage mixed with sage. I devoured the meal of red, sizzling ham with hot biscuits and gravy cooked with fresh, rich milk. The heaping bowls of vegetables formed by the garden's loam and berries picked from a shaded hollow satisfied my long day's hunger. I dismissed my present reality and journeyed back to one I knew so well.

I felt the change from winter stings seep into the warm approach of unveiling spring. Then the long, strenuous days in blazing-summer sun unfurled in a deliberate pace into autumn's lustrous reward.

I heard the rooster crowing, the rumbling thunder and then pure silence. I heard birds singing in every tree and the mother ewe anxiously bleating for her straying lamb. I heard my grandfather's purposeful command, "It's time you sheared a sheep." He was that way; the sooner a boy learns how to work like a man, he understands why and how to feed his sheep.

My journey took me back as if I'd been reborn in another time and place I knew so well. The seed was firmly implanted and grew to a healthy state. Growing up immersed in and nourished by nature's strength endures without escape.

The year was 1947. Through previous years of sacrifice, my family had struggled through the Great Depression and World War II. Some of our sons, brothers and uncles did not return, but for those who did, it was a time for the promise and realization of better days and better times. It was the dawning of rapid progress in mechanization, technology and communications (imagine life without television). I grew up learning to farm as it was practiced for centuries, essentially working by using our hands to stir the earth, labor in harmony with the expectation that this will be a good year.

It was like a day at the office behind a desk, except each day we were behind our horses pulling mowers, wagons and plows. Horses can't pitch hay, milk 20 cows twice a day, chop the weeds from acres of crops or save a lamb. It takes the touch of a shepherd's heart and hands.

I helped my grandfather that day he patiently worked to save a lamb. I am there today. The opening paragraph of *Feed My Sheep:*

"My granddad took his well-worn pocketknife out of his overall's pocket, pulled out the largest razor-sharp blade and slid it under the dead lamb's skin. A cold sleet beat against the hill and against our faces as his claw-like hands sliced out a section of cold and slimy wool-covered skin from the lamb's back. He needed a portion of the skin large enough to be tied over the back of a live lamb. My granddad knows how to save most every lamb. Some didn't make it, but he always does his best to keep even the frailest ones alive. For some reason known only to him, he seems to care for his sheep more than any other animal on our farm."

With the skin in his hand, he began walking up the hill toward the barn as the forsaken ewe, smelling the scent from the skin of her newborn lamb, followed him with mournful cries. But he knew how to save most every lamb, to give it life. He tied the skin on another lamb, which had been rejected, or had lost its mother. In most similar situations, the mother ewe following him would sniff the skin tied to another and claim it as her own.

Nearing the top of the hill, he stopped, turned and told me to throw the dead lamb in a hollow. Deeply saddened, I had been standing there as if frozen in place thinking about why life or death is such a chance. When I picked up the dead lamb, the one consolation—its little face seemed at peace. When I slung it to the cold barren earth, drops of blood splattered against my face. Stunned and cold, I wiped my face on a sleeve and walked toward the barn; my grandfather needed me. It was warm and cozy where we fed our sheep. Their bleating songs of gratitude were as a happy chorus ringing throughout the barn.

Another passage was quoted in books by two well-known authors, Wendell Berry and RoseAnne Coleman, as follows:

"When you see that you're making other things feel good, it makes you feel good, too. The feeling inside sort of just happens, and you can't say this did it, or that did it. It's the many little things. It doesn't seem that taking sweat-soaked harnesses off tired, hot horses would be something that would make you notice. Opening a barn door for the sheep standing out in a cold rain, or throwing a few grains of corn to the chickens are small things, but these little things begin to add up in you, and you can begin to feel that you're important. You may not be real important like people who do great things that you read about in the paper, but you begin to feel that you're important to all the life around you. Nobody else knows or cares too much about what you do, but if you get a good feeling inside about what you do, then it doesn't matter if nobody else knows. I do think about myself a lot when I'm alone way back on the place bringing in the cows or sitting on a mowing machine all day. But when I start thinking about how our animals and crops and fields and woods and gardens sort of all fit together, then I get that good feeling inside and don't worry much about what will happen to me. The best feeling to have is that everything is going to work out."

Writing as a 13-year-old and following up the above quote, I wrote, "It's about as hard to explain feelings as it is to explain how the cherry blossoms turn to sweet cherries on the tree behind the smokehouse." Describing one's deeper feelings is difficult at any age.

A portion of the book was also used as an article in the Mobile Bay Monthly titled "Country Kind of Life." The passages used explain this thought. "I have mixed feelings when I think about how hard farm life can be. And yet, I feel so free and easy in a way, whenever I stop for a moment and think how it has a hold on me..."

In a comment about the book, I wrote: "The book is about the boy's evolving recognition of his grandfather's soul and the discovery of his own." On one occasion, when I was reading and discussing a few passages with an audience, I read one, which I had not particularly noticed before, but it seemed to best define the character of my grandfather. The passage describes preparing for dinnertime:

"Some farm women use a big dinner bell in the back yard to let the men know when it's dinnertime, but we always eat at 12:00 o'clock. At dinnertime, we take the workhorses to water, put them in their stalls, and give them a few ears of corn and then head for the house. They get to start eating their dinner before we do, but it's like that. You take care of everything else and then take care of yourself."

My grandfather took good care of his sheep, his land, his family, friends and community all his life. It was his way of taking care of himself.

After writing the last word of my first book and decisively striking the period key, I rolled my chair back from the desk and sat there stunned. My emotions and feelings were muddled with flashes of relief, pride, elation and gratitude. The closing of the book opened a whole new aspect of my life that had been delayed and repressed. When my creative urge was unleashed, commitment and engagement replaced lethargy and aimlessness. Whatever I'm doing—recreational activities, goofing off, fixing a leaky faucet—the little devil in my head pricks me and says, "Go write." I didn't retire to have guilt feelings.

Although it took 34 years, I finally completed the book. Now what? Retire? Not yet, so I began selecting and arranging 71 of my articles for another book, *How Did Back Then Become Right Now?* How did back then become right now? Who knows what now is? I don't, but it's ridiculous, absurd and funny, or most of it is. After publishing the book, I followed the advice of acclaimed actor John Malkovich. When asked if he was satisfied with his past accomplishments, he replied, "No, I don't feel satisfaction, I feel next."

Maybe this time I could make something up. *Briny's Gift* is a work of fiction. The advantage of writing fiction is that it's not as strange as truth. Simply create some characters and a plot, and that's it. The fun part of writing fiction is relying on your imagination and allowing it to set the course. Imagine writing a story about "It's better to give than to receive," and relate it to the Christmas story. I had the theme.

I have no idea how novelists do it, but I do understand that a work of fiction is based on something. A subject is researched, or based on one's experiences. Research is too much work. You have to go to a foreign country and look up stuff that happened in the 17th century. I went back home to the people I grew up with.

On our farm, we had two small houses, more like shacks, where our tenants or sharecroppers lived. In the 1930's, several of these families moved from the coal mines in Appalachia to escape the ravages of the Great Depression. These families lived meagerly from day to day and had little, if any, formal education. To use a plow, hoe and ax requires no schooling. I worked in the fields with these humble, happy folk nearly everyday. They had little materially, but sharing and giving came natural.

I knew families like the fictional Jackson family. From my experiences, I created Harley and Mabel Jackson and their five children. The family lived in a three-room house back on a ridge, equipped only with the barest necessities. They didn't have a radio, telephone, newspapers or books except an old family Bible used primarily to keep records of births, marriages and deaths. Harley could sign his name on those rare occasions when necessary, but his ability to read was suspect, although he occasionally flipped through some of the children's school-books, pausing at the pictures.

Briny, the youngest son at age 12, was bright, loved to read when he wasn't working and brought home books on the two or three days each week he went to school. In spring, summer, and fall, he'd read them out under the shade tree in the yard. When his daddy began wandering out to take a rest and a smoke, Briny wondered why his daddy kept hanging around where he was reading. It bothered him so one day he got the courage to ask, "Do you want me to read a story to you?" His daddy squirmed a bit and then said, "You can if you want to." At work in the fields the day after hearing a Mark Twain story the night before, Briny's daddy talked more than he ever had.

In reference to "It's better to give," Leo Tolstoy said of the peasant class, "If you want to find an example to follow, you should look among the simple, humble folk." It took nearly a year for the son to give a precious gift to his daddy. On Christmas Eve in 1940, they were sitting by the fire. Briny opened the Bible to the Christmas story, and handed it to his daddy, who read about the shepherds tending their flock.

Is there a danger of over-using your mind when your aging body begins shutting down? Can it cause an imbalance? Or put another way, does a weakened, tired body contribute to blankness in you brain? It's like asking, which goes first, your eyes, ears or teeth? Having conducted research on myself, I've found no correlation between running at a gazelle's pace reduced to that of a turtle, and the capacity to write more words.

Former vice-President Dan Quayle famously addressed the mind. He said a mind is wasteful. Or, was it a mind is a terrible thing to waste, like they do in Washington?

It's terribly exhausting to engage one's mind pushing, shoving and coaxing it to design, form and create. I know when my mind rebels, I give it a break and transfer remaining energies to my body and let it write another story like the one I discovered at K2, the second tallest mountain in the world.

CHAPTER 6

IT WILL TAKE YOUR BREATH AWAY

❖ ❖ ❖

A friend told me the last thing she would ever want to do when retiring is to acclimatize anywhere in the world other than on a beach under a palm tree. OK, so go swat mosquitoes, blister in the sun and take turns as the designated shark watcher. Not all retirees should climb mountains, but all retirees should "up" their bodies in whatever way they choose. Pushing and working the old bag of bones a little each day will work wonders.

This chapter is about what you should do with (or to) your body during retirement. Basically, it's only two things—diet and exercise. It means watching what you eat from cans and getting off your can.

Seneca believed that old age was an incurable disease. Robert Hutchins, former president of the University of Chicago, often thought about exercising, but explained, "Whenever I feel like exercising, I lie down until the feeling passes." Maurice Chevalier quipped, "Old age isn't so bad when you consider the alternative." The alternative is to let your body deteriorate, and then your friends get a bit of exercise serving as your pallbearers.

These are my rules for maintaining the body:

1.   *If you've lost it or losing it, find it.*
2.   *When you gain it or if you have it, keep it.*

Without regular exercise, I feel drowsy, lethargic and stressed. After a brisk five-mile run, I feel refreshed, relaxed and rested. I'm crazy. No, well, maybe in other ways, but vigorous physical exercise is relaxing. An unused body is like an old rusty lawn mower that you crank and crank, and it only sputters. Sharpen the blades, re-fuel it and tune it up a bit and it will cut grass. Keeping your body fit eliminates grass growing under your feet, which would soon grow up to your knees, thus preventing them from bending.

I continue to be amazed at the human body and its capabilities. The age-old adage—if you don't use it, you lose it—holds true. If you haven't used it all that much, why start now when you need to need time to spend your Social Security checks? Being secure socially is not enough. You can't spend the checks if you can't walk through a mall.

To keep the cardiovascular and respiratory systems healthy and fit, the American Heart Association recommends a minimum of 30 minutes of vigorous exercise three times per week. To assist in increasing one's life span, the experts recommend a minimum of 60 minutes of vigorous exercise three times per week. In talking with friends—old and young—about the thirty-minute minimum rule, the usual reply is "I know I should, but I don't have time." Who does? There are 168 hours in a week. Put on the sweats, exercise vigorously for 30 minutes and take a shower three times per week. That's a total of about three of 168 hours per week, and you can't find the time? Physical exercise is particularly important for retirees because most work required some movement of the body. If nothing else, you had to walk from the parking lot to the office. The experts claim that a sedentary existence causes as much heart damage as smoking a pack of cigarettes each day. If you do smoke, all the more reason to go to the Himalayas where Marlboros are as rare as the abominable snowman.

After an exhausting, draining day at work, I'd usually go home and crash. An hour on the couch staring at the stupid TV provided the strength to maneuver to the dinner table and then back to the couch. I changed the routine. After work, I began jogging and running for up to an hour. I'd go home feeling revitalized and dinner was delicious and sleep sweet.

Fortunately, I've been lucky and blessed with good health for 76 years and have been physically active from the day I learned to walk. I never missed a day at work because of illness. Growing up on a hill farm with my grandfather, I practically walked and ran from sunup to sundown. At daybreak, I'd go fetch the horses and cows from the field, then follow a plow, pitch hay and round up and run after stray cattle and sheep. That was my daily routine.

On Sunday afternoons after being cleansed at the Short Creek Baptist Church and then dinner at a table loaded with bowls of vegetables from the garden and fried chicken or cured country ham, or both, with gravy and biscuits, I'd be ready for some baseball in the barn lot or shooting hoops at the basket nailed to the dairy barn. My farm-boy friends would gather every Sunday afternoon with some type of old beat-up ball and we'd play until milking time. The old folks obeyed the Sabbath day of rest by resting under shade trees and on front porch swings.

I loved playing basketball and played from the time I could hold a ball through college and for the Amphibious Force team in the Navy. What's the connection of playing basketball with defending our country? It helps boost morale. And to boost my morale, I played basketball with the boys at school during my working days until I was in my mid-fifties.

In Paul's letter to Timothy, 4:8, he writes, "Bodily exercise profiteth little, but Godliness is profitable unto all things." I don't agree. When Paul wrote it, he probably disregarded walking through the Holy Land nearly every day. Why can't we profit both our body and our Godliness? Exercising my body, although slightly painful in a way, is easier than exercising my spirit. Keeping my weight down is easier than keeping my soul in shape. Isaiah writes in 35:3, "Strengthen the weak hands and make firm the weak knees." That is why I run, to firm up my week knees while struggling to attain Godliness.

You can run most anywhere, but it's tough running up to Mt. Everest. Katmandu, Nepal is an excellent place to begin the first retirement adventure.

It's an historic, quaint, exotic and fascinating small city with more Buddhist and Hindu temples and shrines per square mile than any other city in the world. There are temples on nearly every street. The sacred Bagmati River runs through Katmandu, which is nestled in a valley surrounded by the foothills south of the Himalayas.

It takes months to prepare for a month-long "Ultimate Trek to Everest." A trek is a long walk or hike requiring the necessary equipment and supplies which can take several weeks. To arrange these type trips, you can go it alone or with a companion and follow your own schedule. It's much cheaper that way and many younger people choose to roam abroad during long breaks from school, or before roaming through the mountainous corporate world.

There are several private businesses sponsoring all kinds of adventurous trips throughout the world. I've used three different ones, and all performed their services professionally and took very good care of their clients. Of course, you pay them, but the services for up to a month or longer are reasonable considering the travel, equipment, food and accommodations involved. I signed on for an "ultimate" trek to Everest with Wilderness Travel, located in Berkley, California. They do an excellent job planning, organizing and conducting trips, treks and adventures throughout the world. I used their services on three other occasions.

Several months before the trek, Wilderness Travel began sending vital information, including a list of books about the area, the trip itinerary, names and addresses of the traveling group, travel plans, plane tickets, equipment and clothing lists and enough medical information to prepare one for med school.

To begin the trek, our group, consisting of seven men and seven women from all parts of the U.S., assembled at the Shangri La Hotel in Katmandu. Close friendships began forming at the first meeting, and after 18 years, I continue to have contact with some members of the group. Frances Klatzel our guide, had previously spent three months living in the Himalayan area.

The Shangri La is a quaint little hotel with a beautiful flower garden adjoining the restaurant. It was an excellent place to relax in the warm sun after 28 hours traveling to get there. We lost a day traveling half way around the world. I've lost a lot of days in my time, but have yet to understand how one can actually lose a complete day like losing car keys.

When I give presentations or conduct discussions about my trips, I'm invariably asked about the food, the people, and safety. Most Holiday Inn type people also want to know if the bathrooms are clean and sanitized. Considering the circumstances, the food on the trek was quite good with the exception of yak tongue, which was tough and spongy. We had to chew it like a contented cow chewing her cud. But it was rather amazing how Pemba, one of our Sherpas and our cook, could open a couple duffle bags, take out some pans and food and cook a hearty and, usually, tasty meal in a small tent using a kerosene stove.

The people were wonderful, and we were safe unless falling off a mountain, or a war broke out as it did in Kashmir when I was there on the Ladakh trek. India and Pakistan became irritated with each other again, and we were stuck in a camp for three days before the gunfire ceased.

Going to the bathroom to eliminate is natural like eating, drinking and reproduction. On the trail, the bathrooms were located either behind a rock, a tree or out in the wide-open spaces. They were crude, but sanitized, because if the sun can fry your skin, what do you think it does to germs? When nature rang my bladder bell about every half hour, I went anywhere I wanted and kept going and going. In high altitude, we had to drink water as a camel does at an oasis. Altitude causes dehydration, and one must drink about four times the amount of water normally consumed. Four liters per day of liquids was the minimum. On the trail, shout "Bathroom!" and veer off the trail and lag behind. Some of the women wore long, heavy skirts over their trekking pants to provide a bit more privacy when squatting. It didn't take long to learn to respect everyone's privacy. If watching people go to the bathroom is one of your quirks, you'd travel alone.

At camps, a teepee-type tent with a deep hole in the center was the commode. We'd go there when the urge hit and do our business, and then rake some dirt over the waste and use a cigarette lighter to burn the paper. We also used the lighter to burn waste paper on the trail and to light our candle lantern in the tent, which provided light and about enough heat to warm one finger.

Were the showers warm? No, the showers were back at the hotel. Then how did we keep our bodies clean and change into fresh clothes every day for three weeks? We didn't, but we got used to it with our grimy friends looking the same. Talk about one of life's pleasures! After three weeks collecting dirt and grime, we checked back in at the Shangri La, removed our putrid clothing and stood under precious hot water scrubbing off the scum.

At daybreak each day, the porters brought a basin of warm water to our tents and hot tea or coffee. The first reaction upon being awakened while snuggled deep in a warm sleeping bag is, "Oh, I'm late for work. No, I'm not. I'm retired with not a care in the world other than moving my aching bones up the next steep mountain." But it was a beautiful, wonderful new day and we'd rinse the exposed body parts, forgetting about what's underneath. Another equipment necessity was a large pack of baby wipes used for a temporary sponge bath, and much better than plunging in an icy-cold mountain stream.

Were the Laundromats handy? Yes, they were right around the corner. Occasionally, we'd take a rest day, walk to the nearest washtub, which was a roaring stream, throw some underwear, socks and a shirt or two in the water and let God's agitator cleanse them. The problem was that it took about three days for clothes to dry at high altitude, so forget clean clothes; God loves both the sinner and the unclean, and protects the feeble minded. I did try changing to clean socks and underwear occasionally. Nothing like clean socks; Winston Churchill changed his two or three times each day and he didn't walk all that much. We'd wash our socks and underwear in a stream, put them in a mesh bag, tie it to our packs to help them dry during the day and then hang them in our tents at night.

What about Happy Hour? At the end of a long trekking day, we'd stumble into the dining tent and gulp down several hot cups of tea and some stale crackers serving as appetizers. Martinis were forbidden and we didn't want to burden a yak with an open bar. Alcohol at high altitude will dehydrate you faster than a blast furnace.

There are two ways to get from Katmandu to Lukla, which was the departing point for trekking to Mt. Everest. The boundary line separating Nepal, at the south, and Tibet, at the north, goes directly over the peak of Everest. One way is to walk up through and over the mountains for two weeks; the other is to fly for 45 minutes on a jumbo 16-passenger Nepali Airlines twin-engine plane. After going to the airport to depart for Lukla and waiting for three hours for take-off, the flight was cancelled. The daily flight to Lukla departs only during early mornings due to strong winds that increasingly blow through the mountains as the day progresses. Our flight was cancelled due to unsafe morning winds. You ain't seen weather yet until you get close to Everest.

We returned to the hotel, but there was no room in the inn—heard that before? We were transferred to the acclaimed Yak and Yeti Hotel, which is the Waldorf Astoria of Katmandu. My room, ornately trimmed with woodcarvings, was designed and carved by an indigenous sect known as Newars. They also carved many doors, windows and trim on other buildings in Katmandu. Newars are regarded as perhaps the most skilled and finest wood carvers in the world.

Early the next morning, we returned to the airport. The 15 of us crammed into the 16-seat plane and departed. I sat directly behind the pilot, which was not a smart move, because I could see where we were going. You've ridden roller coasters haven't you with their dips and doodles? But the scenery was awesome, a fairyland with peaks and spires, laced and layered with pure-white snow, reaching for the heavens above gray-granite walls and steep slopes of emerald green. The roaring streams deep in the valleys cast sparkling gems into misty veils cleansed by the crisp sun. Breathtaking! To reiterate George Carlin's observations, "It's not how many breaths you take; it's how many times your breath is taken away."

Landing a small airplane on a dirt and rock covered runway carved out of a mountainside may induce vomiting, but after your spasms subside, the scenery is unbelievable. So when retiring, you may want to fly to Lukla; here's how to get there.

I'd read about the airstrip in downtown Lukla, a village of about a couple hundred Nepali natives. As we wove our way around, up, over, down and through the highest mountain range on earth, I spotted the landing area. From the air, it looked like a Band-aid stuck on the side of an elephant. The landing strip was on the side of a mountain, and mountains are not designed with level spaces. I turned on my video camera, and from directly behind the pilot's head, aimed it at the dusty, rocky landing strip. When we bounced off Mother Earth with dust flying, the plane was heading up a steep incline. The pilot abruptly turned the plane sharply to the right before it slammed into the side of the mountain. When he cut the motor off, our group shouted in unison, something like "Glory Halleluiah" to God's answer to our prayers. Death on the eighth day of my retirement would have been like food poisoning on my honeymoon.

Although not recorded, God undoubtedly said, "Let there be beautiful, high mountains for man to ponder, but not to climb. If man attempts going up, I will deprive him of oxygen, which will smite him down, and he shall suffereth sores on his lungs and in his head." God keeps his promises.

When I stepped out of the plane and looked up at the mountains, my reaction was the same as the response described by Francis Younghusband, an early explorer to the Himalayas in 1924: "As I stepped out on my first day in the Himalayas, a strange exhilaration thrilled me. I kept squeezing my fists together and saying emphatically to myself and to the universe at large: 'Oh, yes! Oh, yes! This really is splendid. How splendid! How splendid!'

The porters unloaded our gear from the plane and tied the duffle bags on dzos, which are a cross between a cow and a yak. The altitude was too low for yaks; we'd use them later. The altitude at Lukla is 9,380 feet. We put on our daypacks and began walking up and up to an altitude of 18,450 feet a few days later. During the next 21 days, my Hilton was a tent with a plush sleeping bag, but the heating system didn't work as the temperature dropped at night to single digits.

A daypack contains only what is needed for the day. Another large backpack and duffle bag stuffed with our gear was slung and tied over the backs of beasts. The rule for any high altitude adventure is to pack only the absolute essentials. A daypack for a day's trek always contains layers of extra clothing, thick sunglasses, about a pint of sunscreen, two liters of water and sometimes lunch. Some days, a porter goes ahead of the group and prepares a hot lunch midway through the day's trek. Other items, such as cameras, a book and journal, snacks, an umbrella can be carried, but one soon learns that carrying an extra pound takes off five extra fat pounds and reduces the legs to rubber.

From Lukla, the next stop was Namche Bazaar, which is 11,250 feet. How did we get there? We walked there slowly, like a snail with a sprained ankle running the Kentucky Derby. Perhaps you've driven through the Rockies, stopped the car at 8,000 feet, took a little walk and felt like somebody turned your fuel pump off. It was like I left my fuel pump back in the states.

About the only worry going up is catching altitude illness. However, it would be worse falling to a lower altitude. High altitudes cause a condition like having jet lag, a hangover and the Asian flu all at the same time. Some of the symptoms are severe headaches, nausea, lethargy and disorientation. It affects the stomach, lungs, blood, urine, nose, legs, feet, the head and what's inside it. Altitude also causes an attitude, which is not good. The major cause of altitude illness is going too high too fast.

When climbing to the clouds, the body has to oxygenate and the breathing rate has to increase, even while at rest. This extra ventilation increases the oxygen content in the blood, but not to sea level concentrations. Since the amount of oxygen required for activity is the same, the body must adjust to having less oxygen. In addition, for reasons not entirely understood, high altitude and lower air pressure cause fluid to leak from the capillaries, which can cause fluid build-up in both the lungs and brain. If it becomes excessive, you can develop pulmonary and/or cerebral edema, a very serious physical condition. Continuing on to higher altitudes without proper acclimatization can lead to potentially serious, even life-threatening illness. What happens then? You must be taken down rapidly to a lower level, or you die and are buried in a glacier. Of course, normal people think that when friends get the urge to see what it's like up there, they already have a significant amount of fluid on their brain.

Climbers and trekkers acclimatize at different rates, and altitude affects people in different ways. A big strong tackle for the Packers might have much more difficulty than a lithe young Dallas Cowboy cheerleader would. Fortunately, I adjusted better than most, but going up is always tough. My experience is that the difference in age makes little difference. A 60-year old might acclimatize and adapt to higher altitudes easier than a 20-year old.

Generally, it takes a minimum of five days of ascension to acclimatize to altitudes of around 15,000 feet and above. If starting at 10,000 feet, one should gain no more than 1,000 to 1,500 feet per day. Acclimatizing to climb Everest and the highest mountains takes weeks. Climbers practice what's known as "climbing high and sleeping low." They climb to 24,000 feet, sleep, take half their gear to 25,000 feet the next day, go back down and sleep. They repeat this procedure until they're standing on the peak. I followed this procedure trying to climb Aconcagua in Argentina, the highest mountain in the western hemisphere, when I was younger at 71. I'll let you know how it turned out in a later chapter, which may be titled— "Are You Sure You Have A Death Wish?"

Flying halfway around the world affects the body in various ways, particularly sleep patterns, the head and the stomach. You grab a burger meal before takeoff and adjust to Katmandu food upon landing. The stomach immediately announces, "French fries, yes; dhal baht, no." This dish is a spicy lentil sauce over rice, so get used to it. Dhal baht and variations are a staple in many Asian countries, and the natives thrive on it.

We began the trek with uncooperative stomachs and confused and reluctant bodies. It feels like you've swallowed rotten eggs and then been mugged. On our first day out and up, one of the ladies became so weak we had to help her along by holding her hand and pulling her up. I overdid it and paid the price. That night my head felt as if it would explode. I seldom ever have headaches, but that night I would have traded my head for the headaches caused by a school full of kids. However, after three or four days, my body and everyone else's in the group began becoming stronger and tougher. The body is amazing; what a gift!

In the Himalayas, trekking and climbing opportunities occur only during spring and fall. Winter there is like Antarctica and summer is the monsoon season. Warm air rises from the Indian Ocean, sweeps up across the plains meets the high mountains and dumps torrents of rain throughout the summer months.

Most days are nice and relatively warm, but the nights turn cold, especially the higher one goes. When the sun comes up, it's like turning up a thermostat. I was trekking along once wearing only pants and a shirt. When I stopped in the shade of a cliff for a rest break, I noticed a sudden temperature change and looked at my thermometer; it was 28 degrees. It can fall to zero at night, and that's what sleeping bags are for. Getting out of them wakes you up.

A typical trekking day began at daybreak with "bed tea," when our porters delivered hot tea or coffee to our tents. This custom goes back to the British days when they were colonizing the world, or trying to. I tried adopting this procedure when I returned home, but my wife refused to become a Sherpa. Our porters always tried to help and assist us at all times anyway they could. They were eager, kind and considerate. Most were Buddhists, and compassion for all living creatures is their creed. Most all other religions talk about compassion, but it's a Buddhist way of life. Not only did they carry very heavy loads, often barefoot, over rough terrain in all kinds of weather, they took care of the tents and camps, cooked the food and scrubbed the pots and pans. What more could you expect for $3 per day?

After breakfast in a larger dining tent, we'd pack our daypacks and prepare for a hard day at the office, which was God's glorious and breathtaking outdoor complex minus computer terminals. After we departed for the day, the porters broke camp, loaded the animals and usually passed us along the way, and had the next camp set up at the end of the day.

And God said, "Let the earth bring forth living creatures according to their kinds: cattle and creeping things and beasts of the earth…. And God saw that it was good." It was good we had beasts, not creeping things, to carry our heavy loads. Dzos and yaks in the Himalayas, ponies in Ladahk and camels on the trek up to K2 on the China-Pakistan border carried our loads. In Bolivia, we depended on llamas and in Argentina, mules. Having grown up on a farm with all kinds of animals—well, not llamas, yaks and camels—I especially appreciated and continue marveling at the unique place animals have and their contributions to our lives on earth.

The beasts of burden cannot go everywhere that man can go. You don't rope a mule and have him pull himself up a steep wall of ice. Therefore, you become a beast of burden and this is when the fun starts. Carrying your own gear up to 18,000 feet requires the strength of a mule.

The most important items in our daypacks were two forms of liquid, water and sunscreen. At higher altitudes, the sun could burn us to a crisp, and blind us without the highest quality wrap-around sunglasses. At one point, the sun was so bright I wore two pair. Usually, all parts of the body were covered with clothing except the face and hands after the day warmed. We then periodically rubbed the strongest sunscreen on exposed parts, including inside our ears and up our noses. If not, the sun would reflect from the ice and snow and burn the insides of our noses. Lip balm was as important to us as lipstick is to a prostitute. I once forgot to rub sunscreen on my hands and burnt the backs of them so badly they looked liked singed sponges.

Don't drink the water once you leave JFK. Water helps keeps you alive, but it can also kill. Purified water is available in bottles in most countries now, but wasn't always the case. We were warned to inspect the top of every bottle of water in restaurants, because in some places they'd refill the bottles from the tap.

To prevent dehydration on the trek, we continuously drank water plus cups and cups of broth and tea at the camps. This intake requires about 15 trips behind a rock each day, which should be as high as your waist if you're reasonably modest.

I always kept a plentiful supply of water purification tablets on trips abroad. These tablets contain iodine, which doesn't taste like the lemons or hops which are brewed into other popular liquids. A neutralizer tablet added after the iodine takes effect made our water taste a bit better, but not like water at home.

Don't brush your teeth with tap water in developing countries and don't drink beverages with ice. On my first trip to Everest, after a few squeamish stomach days initially, I suffered very few sickly days on the trek. When we arrived back at the hotel, we celebrated with alcohol, which will practically kill most every germ. I forgot to remove the ice until the drink was half finished and then had to hang around a bathroom for a day or two.

On some treks, the porters boil the water, but if two liters don't last during a trekking day, and they won't, then you use the iodine tablets or a small water filter, which takes time to process. On a trip climbing in the Andes in Argentina, our guide insisted we drink water from the streams. He believed that iodine tablets would not only kill the germs in the water, but also those "good" germs in our stomachs, which naturally fight against illness. He said there was no purer water on earth than that cascading down from the mountains. So I'd stick my water bottles in a roaring, grayish, gritty stream and drink. It must have been the grit in the water bombarding the germs into submission.

Don't get discouraged yet about your first month of retirement. You need not follow my example. Consuming margaritas on a beach is another way to prevent malaria.

Was the food good and was it fast? Yes, it was. It was like you've had a hard day at the office, missed lunch and, being famished, stopped at a drive thru for a burger on the way home for dinner. Walk over high mountains all day long burning a zillion calories, and then stagger into a dining tent at dinnertime, and you'll be hungry enough to eat a yak.

Breakfast usually consisted of hot porridge, occasionally powdered scrambled eggs and some type of bread or chapattis with jam and peanut butter. When we carried our own lunches, it included tins of some type of meat or tuna, and hunks of cheese and crackers. Dinners were served with tasty soups and were heavy on potatoes and rice covered with lentils or other spicy sauces, and these dishes were prepared in various ways. The fold-up table in the dining tent was usually set with Tang, cocoa, powdered milk, salt, pepper, sugar, jam, peanut butter, catsup, chili and garlic sauce and black or green tea. Some fresh meat, including water buffalo, was served early during the trek. In Ladakh the ponies actually carried baskets of live chickens and we had eggs every day and roast chicken toward the end of the trek. During that trek, our guide, Hugh Swift, a great guy, who had written the definitive book on trekking, *The Trekkers Guide to the Himalaya and Karokoram,* purchased a sheep from a shepherd. In keeping with their reverence for all sentient beings, our Buddhist porters were not responsible for slaughtering the sheep. Our Muslim porters did and we had mutton dishes for the next few days. What helped to make that trek so enjoyable with Hugh was his enthusiasm and pure joy in traipsing through the mountains, which to him was a heavenly place.

A couple of years after that trek, I learned that Hugh had met a tragic death. He had spent the summer months for several years roaming, trekking and climbing in that part of the world and faced numerous dangerous situations. He once fell nearly a hundred feet into a deep crevasse on a glacier, but eventually was rescued by his companion. During winters, Hugh returned to his home in Berkeley. During his last visit, he went to get his yearly physical checkup. The doctor performed a minor procedure, but, apparently, the effect of the medicine caused him to faint when he walked out on the street. He died when he fell and hit his head on the curb.

The food was good on my treks and mountain-climbing expeditions, considering the circumstances. All the food, stoves and cooking utensils had to be slung across the backs of pack animals and transported for weeks. When we went higher or to places the pack animals could not go, we'd carry the food and gear, which doubled the fun.

It was rather amazing how Pemba, one of our Sherpas and our cook, could put together a hearty and tasty meal in a small tent. He was full of surprises. At the famed Tengboche Monastery (Buddhists call them gompas) high up near the base of Mt. Everest, he served an apple pie that would have made Aunt Minnie envious. Three years later when we met our Sherpas in Lhasa in preparation for a journey through Tibet, Pemba was there with his pots and pans.

As mentioned earlier, our next stop was Namche. We arrived there on a Friday in time for the bazaar on Saturday. Namche is a village of a couple hundred Nepalis and set on a horseshoe-shaped mountainside with spectacular peaks hovering above. Saturday was shopping day at the outdoor market as the natives gathered from the surrounding areas to bargain for wares—shoes, pans, rice, spices and trinkets. The meat market was popular, with sides of dried goat carried in by Tibetans. All goods were carried for miles. On the trail, we'd give way to workers carrying everything from lumber to sacks of rice. They'd bring heavy loads over rugged terrain, and I struggled with a 20-pound daypack.

After an interesting two days in Namche, we made our way toward the Tengboche Monastery. A four-inch snow had fallen the night before. One travel writer described Tengboche, where 40 monks reside, as one of the most spectacular settings on earth. It rests beneath the spreading arms of Ama Dablam, the "Mother's Charm Box" at 22,494 feet. We could see the tip of Mt. Everest's peak hidden behind the Lhotse-Nuptse 26,000-foot wall. When we were there, the monastery had burned two years earlier and was being rebuilt. The monks had been convinced to have a generator installed at a nearby stream to provide electric lighting for the ancient monastery. When the generator caught fire, it burned the monastery. The new monastery was under construction, but no thanks, instead of installing sockets for light bulbs, the monks would rely on hundreds of flickering butter lamps placed around the temple. This type of light would provide a more conducive atmosphere in the quest to attain enlightenment.

Who says the yeti, abominable snowman or "Big Foot" are myths? They're not, because I saw a yeti skull. When we were passing through a little village, the keeper at a small Buddhist shrine brought out a wooden box for us to see. He opened the box and it was either a yeti skull or a 15-inch pointed pyramid with reddish-brown hair on top. Scientists analyzed the skull, but never identified the specimen. Is it a bear-ape type thing or some combination with possibly human characteristics? I've seen a few long-pointed-head, furry human beings who behaved abominably. Most every small town has at least one. There are also plaster prints on record of strange, huge footprints from the area, which have not been identified. There have been numerous sightings from reputable sources of large furry creatures lurking in the shadows.

Our guide, Frances, who had previously lived at Tengboche for three months helping to establish a small cultural center and museum, explained that so many areas of the Himalayas are unexplored. She is a skeptic, but doesn't discount the mystical legends and the reality of the magic at the highest part of the earth and closest to the heavens. Whatever the case, I kept my eyes peeled. If I spotted a Big Foot, I'd lasso it, become rich and famous, forget these strenuous treks and climb nothing higher than a sand dune.

If you are worried about what to do during retirement, searching for Big Foot could consume your time and be quite an adventure. Your possibilities are endless. Joseph Conrad explained, "We must be willing to get rid of the life we planned, so as to have the life waiting for us." We make a living and raise a family our first 60 years, and that's about it. The second life waiting for us can become a let-it-happen

series of adventures and experiences that can be
most renewing and rewarding if we light the fuse.

Why risk pulmonary and cerebral edema to see
a mountain? I don't have a clue other than something similar to how George Mallory responded
when asked why he attempted climbing Everest in
1924—"Because it's there." I had no reason other
than I wanted to see it, because it was there. Why go
to the moon or sail a raft made of reeds across an
ocean? But wouldn't it have been much cheaper and
simpler to subscribe to National Geographic? Yes, it
would, but you don't gasp for air reading National
Geographic or lose weight snacking as you turn the
pages.

After eight days of trekking with oxygen cut in
half, our group strengthened and toughened. Most
of our queasy stomachs, blistered feet and blow-the-
top-off-your-head headaches were reduced from "I
can't take it any more" to "Oh, what the hell."

Our goal was to trek to and climb Kala Patar at
18,450 feet, which is considered the most spectacular vantage point to view Mt. Everest. We camped
at a tiny summer shepherd's village called Lobuche
before the final assault. During the cold and black
night, I had my second worst headache of the trip.
When I awoke, I felt extremely weak and quite concerned about the most strenuous day of all. I had
retired, grabbed a plane and strained every fiber,

tissue and vital organ of my body so I could see a gigantic mound of rock. It's the climactic day, and I spend it lying in a tent shivering?

Once I got on my feet and skipped breakfast, I began regaining a measure of strength and joined our group as we made our way from camp up a valley and over the long Khumbu glacier. The glacier had developed over centuries from the thawing and refreezing waters cascading down from the continuous fresh mountains of snow falling on Everest.

We trekked about three miles to the south-face base camp where a team of Koreans was preparing to climb Everest. Kala Patar is known as the Black Mountain, and we had about a 2,000-foot climb to reach the top. A fast runner can cover 2,000 feet in about a minute. With strength recovered and adrenaline pumping, I ran to the top of the mountain in about two hours. At that altitude, take four steps, stop and suck air, take four more steps, stop and ask God why you're being punished.

Eventually, all members of our group made it to the top and celebrated with toasts of iodine water in liter bottles. In the valley 2,000-feet below, the Korean team, like a cluster of busy ants, was preparing to pursue their dream. They would soon begin the treacherous ascent of the nearby Khumbu icefall, and then summit many days later, if their dream didn't turn into a nightmare.

Our tight-knit family group sat on the peak of Kala Patar, elated with our accomplishment. We watched the wind unceasingly blow a thin veil of snow off the peak of Everest. It was a quiet and peaceful place with the only disturbance coming from an occasional raven soaring and cawing at the unwelcome intruders. I sat contemplating why and how I arrived there while absorbing the power emanating from the point on earth closest to the source that created the earth and all the life below and beyond.

How does one describe the scene—the setting and the mountain—other than it's spectacular, magnificent, and over-whelming? If choosing only one descriptive term, it would be POWER. I felt a sense of power, strength and nobility from the mountain, which was both humbling and inspiring. The beauty and power of nature's stupendous forces electrifies and takes one's inner spirit to a higher plane.

Thirteen days earlier, I had begun the journey to fulfill one of my dreams and begin retirement with the trip of a lifetime. Maybe it would be my one and only trip of that kind. But I began having other dreams, even there on the summit. OK, I was hallucinating, and the altitude finally got me. Could I ever climb a mountain using ropes and all the climbing gear? And I wondered what Mt. Everest looked like from the north face in Tibet. I'd heard that K2, the second tallest mountain in the world, was a more dramatic scene than Mt. Everest. Someday, I wanted to run a marathon, but 26.2 miles was too far. And someday I wanted to write a book, but I'd have to sit for 26.2 miles.

During retirement, you'll have more time to dream. Most will be pleasant and peaceful ones like dreaming that your grandchildren think you and God are brothers, or dreams about the gentle salt-water tides soothing your delicate feet as you sip cold drinks building up the appetite to eat banana-sized shrimp. You'll probably also dream some wild, weird and crazy ones. Pay attention to my dream rule for your retirement:

Dream the wild and crazy ones—about something you've always wanted to do—and pursue them with every ounce of whatever you have remaining, which is more than you've ever dreamed.

What goes up must come down, and going down a mountain destroys what's remaining of the two long appendages that have two feet attached. The strain of holding back is torture. There is a point when your legs request you get down on your hands and knees and crawl.

After descending the peak and trekking back down the glacier, it was nearly dark when we all reached camp. In six more days, we'd arrive back in Lukla and the airstrip—oh, God, no. It wasn't that I wanted to remain in the mountains; it was that I'd watched the plane take off after we'd been dumped in downtown Lukla to begin our trip. When the pilot gunned the plane, it seemed to sputter and struggle, kicking up dust and bouncing off the boulders.

With a few feet remaining, the plane would either lift its wings or plunge thousands of feet into the abyss where yetis roam. Weaving and wobbling in the fierce mountain winds, God said, "I don't need you up here yet."

After six days trekking back to Lukla, it was our turn to board the plane. Thankfully, the plane flapped its wings and a couple of hours later we strolled into the Shangri-La Hotel. If you saw a filthy group like our group strolling into a Crown Hilton in America, you'd call security. Oh, the joys of hot water and a bar of soap.

After a couple of days relaxing and seeing some of the fabulous sights in Katmandu, we said our goodbyes. Don't forget to write and stay in touch. We exchanged photographs weeks later, and I sent a copy of my video to each member, which included the loud audio portion of the screams when we touched down in Lukla.

When you retire and take a trip to a strange place, you may get stranded. As my wonderful new friends began flying back to their homes, I remained in Katmandu. Why? When I planned the trip, I thought that if I was going half way around the world for the trek to see a mountain, why not stay a bit longer and see some other sites and places. Maybe I'd take a quick trip to Lhasa in Tibet or to the Annapurna area in Nepal, which is considered a more beautiful area than that surrounding Mt. Everest. It was November 27 and my flight was reserved for December 20.

On second thought, since it will soon be Christmas and family time, I think I want to go home. After all those years with my kids—and the thousands of other people's kids—and then having just completed this demanding and strenuous trip, I could use a bit of rest. I'm worn out. No, I'm not. I'm homesick. No, I'm not. Well, yes, I am. And won't it be a joy to sit back and watch TV again. No, it won't. I went to the Thai Airline office to get an earlier flight, and informed the flights to Bangkok were booked solid during December; but I could check each day for a cancellation.

If you have to be stuck in a place, it could be considerably worse than in Katmandu. At that time, an acceptable hotel room cost less than $12 and a good meal was a couple bucks. The city is filled with ancient and historic sights and the people are incredibly friendly and helpful. At that time, crime or any type of violence was practically non-existent, a tribute to the Buddhist and Hindu ethic and morality.

So, I could perhaps take short trips around the area, wander around the city, read, write, sit in the sun and relax, which would be a new experience. I recorded in my journal:

"I miss home and the comforts there. Perhaps this is training for me—to learn patience and how to relax. With retirement, I now must learn how to use time effectively."

My insight was on the mark. My life's journey leading up to this one had been long, arduous and demanding. It had been a time of never taking time to smell the roses. I had always tried to stay ahead of something, because as Satchel Paige said, "Something might be gaining on you." If I caught a hint of a sweet scent in the air, my sense was to move on to make more cents. Despite a few bumps along the way, my life's journey up to retirement had been most gratifying and rewarding. I've always considered myself one of those luckiest guys.

While waiting around for a ticket to home, one evening during dinner at the Vajra Hotel, a waiter came in and asked for "Cummins." How could I have a phone call? No one on earth knew where I was. I have an understanding with Vera and my family that they're not to worry, and they don't. I won't attempt to analyze why, but my family has become accustomed to my taking seldom-traveled forks on roads leading to who knows where.

"This is Gary McCue and you don't know me."

"Yes, I do. You wrote *Trekking in Tibet.*"

"Yes, I have, and Frances Klatzel told me you were heading back to the states soon." (I'd forgotten I had told our guide that I would be staying at the Vajra until flying home.)

Gary asked, "If you have room, would you mind taking my Christmas cards back to the states and mailing them? From here, you never know if they'll get there."

"I'll gladly take them," I said.

He brought the cards to my hotel along with his newly published book. We talked, and I told him I'd love to see Tibet. He said it was truly an incredible place. It was. Three years later, I went to Tibet, and 11 years after that trip, I met Gary again in Beijing.

"You may not remember me, Gary, but I mailed your Christmas cards from Nepal in 1991." He remembered. And then he took our group all the way across China to the Pakistan and Afghanistan border so we could see K2, the second tallest mountain in the world, OK, so I have a high mountain fetish. It's not sexual like a foot fetish, but perhaps just as strange.

On December 8, Thai Air said I could fly out on the ninth. I'll miss this place. I'll miss my team. One last meal at the Vajra Hotel, and I'd fly out the next day. The Vajra is a small, quaint hotel with a reading room and library containing several ancient books. The hotel was located at the foot of a steep hill, below Swayambhunath, a Buddhist temple, also called The Monkey Temple. The large domed temple with the eyes of Buddha on top cast a protective gaze over the beautiful city and valley below. Nearly every day, I'd walk up the hundreds of steps to the temple where monkeys scampered about. I'd sit in the sun, reading and practicing the art of relaxing. Patience, I learned is indeed a virtue.

The Everest trip was a once in a lifetime experience. Or, it was until three years later, when I went to Tibet and trekked above the advanced base camp at the north face of Mt. Everest, and then that trip was until I trekked above the advanced base camp at K2. Before the K2 trip, I wanted to see if I could climb a mountain using ropes and all the other gear. I did and it was fun, as long as I didn't look down. I'm scared of heights, like what if I fall off a ladder painting ceilings or cleaning my gutters. My wife is into interior design, but I didn't retire to experiment with the color schemes on her walls. Give me the exterior designs far away any day. I'll paint our walls someday—if I get the time.

The family greeted me at the gate, and all was well. Merry Christmas!

What happens when one's life becomes like a coin suddenly flipped? It's an abrupt transformation from a familiar and predictable reality. Work, play, learn and mow the lawn. Turn on the news. There's fighting in Where-is-it-stan, a tornado rips through the plains and a politician announces, we're in a fix.

On the flip side, the only breaking news I heard on the trek were flashes like, "We'll get the best view of Everest today." The reality of the world I knew was temporarily put away. The world I entered became a day-by-day and step-by-step reality. The busy life involving work, family and friends was suddenly replaced with the natural wonders of this fascinating world, which quickly took the cares away. Lifelong habits and routine vanished in a haze. What happened to me? With the mighty mountains hovering over each step I took, my long arduous journey had replenished that which reactivates the source where the inner spirit lies.

Then it's back to the reality of doing menial tasks like taking out the garbage and shaving. Decisions, decisions, do I shave first and take out the garbage sacks, or do the garbage and then lather up? Before our trek ended, all the men had made the decision to shave the three weeks of stubble off when we arrived back at the hotel. Lather freezes on your face shaving at a mountain stream. To prove to my wife I'd actually been in the mountains, I left my razor in the kit. When she saw me, she thought I resembled something between a weary Abe Lincoln and Clint Eastwood in his prime.

Then I had to face my mother, who, when I told her I was going to the Himalayas, wondered where she'd gone wrong with her only son.

"Now you get that stuff off your face right now," she said. I tested her love. My mother continues to love me, even though I haven't shaved since retiring. I don't the have time.

CHAPTER 7

TO CLIMB, OR NOT TO CLIMB

❖ ❖ ❖

"To be, or not to be—that is the question:
Whether 'tis nobler in the mind to suffer
The slings and arrows of outrageous fortune,
Or to take arms against a sea (or mountain), of
troubles,
And by opposing (climbing) them, end them—
or me!
Shakespeare also wrote, "When the age is in, the
wit is out."

You have to be witless to take up mountain climbing at an age when safety experts advise climbing no higher than the third rung of a stepladder. At age 64, when a retiree is standing on a wobbly chair changing a light bulb, you can easily topple off and break a calcium-deficient bone. But at that age, standing on a 20,000-foot summit is much safer. You don't normally tie yourself to ropes when you paint a ceiling.

Climbing up life's rickety ladder is dangerous enough. Reaching the first summit is like carrying four kids in your backpack and climbing 18 years up to a precipice and then tossing them off. Why did I ever get the urge to climb closer to the sky? I do not know, but, why not? When I was in Peru a number of years ago, I remember looking across a valley at one of the beautiful snow-capped peaks and wondering how they ever climb those things? It was a scary thought, and I remember thinking, "Never me." Eleven years later, I stood on top of an Andean peak.

On prior treks to the Himalayas, I observed teams of mountain climbers at various base camps preparing for a challenge like no other; the intoxicating aura of excitement and anticipation is like no other. It's an ultimate blending of body, mind and spirit with the powerful, natural forces. Perhaps such trials and struggles are the means in the long journey to define and conquer oneself.

As mentioned earlier, after reading Peter Mathiessen's *The Snow Leopard,* I wanted to go see the areas he described. After my first journey to the highest mountains, I began reading books about the mountainous areas, trekking journeys through them and the fascinating accounts of climbers' successes, failures and extraordinary feats and experiences. Climbers call it "assaulting" a summit. That's a rather violent connotation. At my age, "uplifting stroll" is a gentler term. I was also captivated watching documentaries about topics such as death on Mt. Everest and how to climb straight up an icefall and love it.

Could I do that? Probably not, but how would I know, unless I gave it a try? Did the notion and desire stem from my competitive nature or my hubris and pride? Was it related to survival of the fittest and the striving and struggle to surpass those

less survivable? Rainer Rilke explained, "All the soar-
ings in the mind begin in my blood." Perhaps there
was no logical explanation for attempting such ven-
tures, except that a puzzling condition kept stirring
in my blood.

Is the urge to climb instinctual? Children climb
before learning to walk. My three boys could crawl to
a window and be half way up a Venetian blind before
I could stop them. If you have young children and
trees in your yard, cut them down—the trees, that is.

In the Bible, there are few references to climbing. The first climbing expedition recorded was
when God called Moses up to the summit of Mt.
Sinai. Going up was not the same burden as carrying
the two heavy stone tablets down and the resulting
aftermath. Amos talks about climbing up to heaven,
which is probably more difficult than climbing Everest blindfolded and without legs. Luke recorded
Zacchaeus climbed a sycamore tree to get a better
view of Jesus. Does this incident have some kind of
religious connection to a father's desire to, "bring
up a child in the way he should go," compelling a
father to build a tree house for his children?

Climbing anything is never easy. One way to
reach the highest place ever created is to do good,
love thy neighbor as thyself, no matter how bigoted
or dumb they are, and to obey the Ten Command-
ments every day. The highest peak on earth is easier
than that.

There is a natural urge to go higher. Monkeys do
it—squirrels and birds, too. Man went to the moon,

and Mars is next. We live in a get-on-a-high culture. When one high wears off, we pursue another. Why shouldn't it apply to retirees? A retiree can escape the lows with drugs, prescription and the other kinds, and most do, but there are ways to attain natural highs—the ones that stay with you. There is a natural inclination to attain a higher plane, and it should not end when Social Security clicks in. Shakespeare, who covered most all facets of the human condition, said, "Tis but a base, ignoble mind, that mounts no higher than a bird can soar." The human condition dictates that when we cease soaring in body, mind and spirit to where the birds fly, a roost becomes our permanent abode.

Prior to my treks in the mountains, I had done little hiking as such. Walking to a destination was too slow for me; running was the way to go. But there was another means of transportation I wanted to try. It's physically challenging, a cheap way to go, and you can take a motel room and restaurant with you. No, it's not an RV, but a backpack, which requires the proverbial weak mind and strong back. Backpacking in a wilderness is an excellent activity providing a good workout and an adventurous experience. Spending a few days strolling through a beautiful natural setting is most rewarding.

My daughter, Dani, was teaching on the Navajo reservation in Northern New Mexico. She coached the Navajo girls in track and cross-country and ran with them over the beautiful wide-open landscape in that area. She was physically fit and well conditioned, having run in the desert and later the New York Marathon.

On weekends, Dani and her friends often traveled to the many canyons in the area and hiked in Chaco, Canyon de Chelle, the Grand Canyon and many other isolated ones.

"Dad, why don't you come out, and we'll backpack the southwest?"

Why not? I borrowed a backpack, flew to Albuquerque and we drove to Hualapai Hilltop, an isolated part of the south rim of the Grand Canyon. From the rim, an eleven-mile trail winds down to the little village of Supai, where the Havasupai tribe lives. That side canyon leading into the grand one is magnificently decorated with bluish-green waterfalls cascading into pools of sparkling emerald water. The summer sun heats the bottom of the Grand Canyon 10 to 15 degrees warmer than the temperature at the top. If it's 90 degrees at the top, you could fry bacon and eggs on a rock at the bottom.

Have you ever done something you didn't know how to do, like properly loading a backpack and putting it on your back so it won't rub the skin off your hips? Despite an aching back and raw hips, Dani and I made it to Supai, cooled off under a waterfall in one of the luminous, blue-green, near perfectly formed pools and pitched our tent. The next morning, we explored the area, packed up and began the eleven-mile uphill climb in scorching sun back to the car.

I learned several valuable lessons during my first backpacking experience. First, I learned how to put a heavy pack on my back without my bone structure becoming twisted and deformed. Secondly, I learned to fill a pack and then throw practically everything out and fill it with 30 gallons of water. Even though Dani and I filled our water bottles before departing Supai, we discovered that after mile four, if we didn't begin rationing this precious life-sustaining substance, the buzzards would have two morsels to pick. We saved one swallow of hot water each to celebrate when sighting the car. After 70 miles of driving over a desolate, rough road, we spotted a Quick Mart oasis and lapped water like two camels in the Sahara.

Dusty, dirty and with our muscles twitching, we drove over 200 miles to the south rim of the Grand Canyon and were revived by long refreshing showers. Upon awakening the next day, my first thought was, "I don't think we can do it." It's difficult to do much of anything if you can't get out of bed. After a day of carrying a backpack eleven miles up a steep incline, the next morning when a leg hits the floor, it wants to buckle. Not indicating my worn and weary condition to my daughter, I said, "Let's go."

It's not that far to hike down to Phantom Ranch across the Colorado River and back up the same day, is it? No, it's not unless you've hiked out of the Havasupai Canyon the day before. We packed lighter loads with some food, water and rain gear and began at the less traveled Kaibab Trail. My plan was to begin the hike, and if the soreness and fatigue were too much to bear, turn back. Why would a runner get sore walking? Different physical activities affect different muscles in different ways.

It was as if we had the Grand Canyon all to ourselves that early beautiful morning. Under a clear blue sky, we descended into a magical and ethereal landscape, a harmonious journey with the sun's deliberate movement and reflections against the steep layered walls. The changing slants of light—tints of purple, green, orange and gold, each viewable moment as strokes brushed by an artist into perfectly layered coats. A walk through time's creation is as a beautifully wrapped gift concealed. My daughter and I untied the bow.

Back to a semblance of reality, it was time for lunch. After crossing the footbridge to Phantom Ranch, we revived our legs and feet in a gentle little brook beside the roaring waters of the mighty Colorado River, always churning and unchanging, its power and strength reviving. And then we got up to complete the day's journey; life's quest never ending, except for those brief, happy, restful pauses that fuel other explorations, and other gifts.

Across another footbridge and up the trail—Bright Angel is the name. Who gave it that name? I envisioned an angel descending and lifting up my spirit from this wondrous chasm, and placing me in a restful heaven above.

The sun had long cast its last ray when Dani and I reached the south rim. Weary at the end of the nearly 18-mile hike, the strenuous, but enchanting walk through time's handiwork, remains embedded in our memories.

A few years later, I agreed to lead three of my children across and through the Grand Canyon. I said cross, meaning north to south. Stupid me, try telling three of your adult children, "You carry this and you carry that." To me, they're still six-year olds. "Daddy doesn't have time to bury you, get down out of that tree this minute!"

With three days' supply of food, tents, sleeping bags, lotions and knick-knacks (water was available at springs), we departed the north rim, the walls of which were about as steep as the outside walls of my house. All went well going down, and as we set up the first camp in a lovely spot and began preparing a delicious freeze-dried dinner, a skunk wandered in to see what was cooking. How do you convince a skunk to empty his bladder a mile away? Gently. "Here kitty, kitty, come this way. Want some jerky, little kitty?"

Late the third day, we reached the south rim and paused to look back at our journey's route. The life-long journey of a family goes in many directions and takes different routes. Those times when family members share the load and travel together are the ones that form and solidify distinct and enduring bonds.

Of all the crazy, moronic, warped things I've tried, experienced and completed/failed since retirement, mountain climbing creates the most interest. Looking for attention from your friends? Go climb a mountain. When I periodically meet acquaintances, invariably I'm asked, "Climbed any mountains lately?" In the present, busy, hectic, cell-phone centered society, who really wants to know what you've been up to? Tell them you've been climbing a mountain, and they'll step back as if you have a deadly disease. For whatever reason, there is a fascination, not necessarily with aspiration, but with aspiring to climb to the top of something often obscured by clouds.

After learning how to pack and carry a backpack and trekking in the highest mountains, I contacted the American Alpine Institute based in Bellingham, Washington. It was another one of my one-thing-leads-to-another escapades. Better than one day leads to a mall walk, the couch and a dinner of fast food.

The American Alpine Institute conducts all types of climbing in various places, and provides instruction for beginners. I was in climber's kindergarten, and had no idea what a crampon was. They sent instructions and a long list of equipment I would need. Some of it was razor sharp and dangerous. You can't climb up an ice wall without daggers on your feet.

After accumulating the required climbing gear, clothing, and necessities, and after getting numerous shots to prevent deadly diseases, I flew to La Paz, Bolivia. This unique city sits down in a bowl-like setting with spectacular mountains surrounding it. At nearly 12,000 feet, La Paz is one of the higher cities in the world. When you walk down the street, it's at a snail's pace. Carry a duffle up one flight of stairs and stop a minute, gasping and wondering where the oxygen went.

After I arrived and met four of the members of our team at the hotel, we went out to dinner. During the meal, I noticed that each of us picked up our fork with the left hand. If it's advantageous for mountain climbers to be left-handed, I'm off to a good start. Scott was a particle physicist and said the majority of particle physicists are left-handed. Did I make a mistake? I could have been working in a cozy laboratory experimenting with particles. Instead, I chose to do something at that point in my life which made me very nervous?

All the groups I've traveled with developed camaraderie, unity, and a realization the success of the goal required a team effort. Our team of eight gelled early into a cohesive family without sibling tension and rivalries. The youngest, 19 year-old Jessica, was a student at Harvard. Cate held a degree from Harvard and had previous climbing experience, as did some of the others. Scott was our physicist and Merle was on the team directing the Hubble telescope mission. Ryan worked in business and Dan manufactured, of all things, large staples. The oldest team member, other than me, was 38-year-old Colin. He owned a farm in Tasmania and grew poppies (legally and under strict security) for a pharmaceutical company. I would soon turn 64 and was kind of a misfit farm boy from the hills of Kentucky. I knew what they were thinking. "Do we take turns pulling the old guy up?"

Our leaders, Brenden and Tim, plus two local guides were experienced climbers. Tim had recently flown to Bolivia from Alaska, where, due to severe weather conditions on a climbing expedition up Mt. McKinley, he'd been trapped in a tent for one week. He had also worked at the South Pole, and on the previous New Year's Day, ran a one-mile race around the pole. "Great guys" is an overused term, but all these guys were great ones.

Some of the taller Andean mountains are only two hours or less from La Paz. We packed our tents, supplies and hiking gear for a five-day hike to acclimatize to the higher altitude. As we were strenuously crossing a 15,000-foot pass, Tim reminded us that we'd go 5,000 feet higher a few days later. Not funny.

After five days acclimatizing, it was back to the hotel for a shower, dinner and a night's rest before the serious stuff. Early the next morning, we tied dozens of duffle bags on the top of a rickety bus and headed for the mountains over rough dirt and rocky roads. It seems unimaginable that at the end of the 20th century, the entire country of Bolivia had only 1,000 miles of paved road. Guess what awaited us at the trailhead? A herd of llamas had volunteered to carry our loads up a scenic valley to the base camp, where the fun began. Ever been in one of those situations where the fun was so abundant, you couldn't stand it?

Early the next morning, Brendan dumped bags of climbing apparatus out on the ground and began a stern lecture. This is a cam, this is a locking carabiner, this is an unlocking carabiner, this is a crampon and on and on to Petzl harnesses, belay ascenders and descenders, quick draws, ice tools, slings and screamers. I wanted to scream.

He continued on, "This is an ice screw. This is a rope, This is…" I raised my hand. "Yes, Terry?"

"I've used those before back on the farm when we roped cattle."

Remember your first day in school? "Now if everyone stays in their seats, we may get to go out and play." Brendan got our attention. During my first day in climbing school, he said, "Pay attention, or you'll die." I stayed in my seat and the next morning at 4:30 a.m., the teacher let us out to play.

How does one learn to climb mountains? It's like making Carnegie Hall—practice, practice. After packing up our climbing gear, we hiked two miles from base camp up to the glacier near the base of Pyramide Blanca. A two-mile hike is a stroll in a park. Well, it's more than that at 15,200 feet, carrying

30 pounds, wearing heavy climbing boots and using a headlamp to light the way. Climbing boots are made of rigid, hard plastic and are large enough to insert a thick, felt liner boot into the outer boot. You put two wool socks on each foot before inserting it into the felt boot. This helps prevent frozen black toes, which means they have to amputate. Once you attach the crampons (spikes) to the outer boots, there's five pounds on each foot. At your lovely home at an altitude of 4,000 feet, if you attach five pounds to each foot, put a 30-pound pack on your back, and go walk around the block, it's naptime or resuscitation.

When we arrived at the ice wall area, I was exhausted and the sun wasn't even up yet. During the hike to get there and begin the important stuff, I needed an hour's break every ten minutes. Brendan reversed it to ten minutes every hour. Oh, well, I'm paying good money for this and I'm stingy.

Practicing crevasse rescue and ice climbing requires your attention. Pretend you've fallen into a deep crack in a glacier—maybe 80 feet deep—and broken only one leg. If you can climb out, you live. Say your roof needs repair, the outside 40-foot wall of your house is made of ice and you don't have a ladder. Simply attach crampons to each foot, take an ice axe and ice hammer and climb up the wall as if you were a squirrel digging little claws into the bark of a hickory tree to retrieve the top nut.

Without going into the technical details of using the two sharp points on the toe end of the crampons and the sharp curved points of the two ice tools, let's just say climbing straight up a 50-foot ice wall is thrilling.

After the first long day of jam-packed climbing school, it was two arduous miles back to camp and nearing darkness, I staggered into my tent, fell on the posture-fitting sleeping bag and noticed that my eyes weren't focusing. The tent door opening was a total blur. I picked up a book and could not read the title on the cover. Do I remain calm, send for a helicopter or pray? Whatever it was, my full vision returned before dinner. This rather alarming condition had never happened during my previous experiences at high altitude and has not occurred since.

Although my CAT (climbing aptitude test) score was quite low, after a second day of climbing school, I became a graduate of what could be considered Dimwit U. Was I ready yet? No, but what was I to do, spend a lonely claustrophobic week in a tent?

The following is part of what I recorded in my journal the day after my first climb:

"July 15, 1999 - my 64th birthday—an incredible day. Hot tea at 4:30 a.m. Had not slept well and somewhat nauseous. Oatmeal at 5:00 and pack up climbing gear, put on heavy boots and head up to the mountain, an exhaustive trek in itself. Put on harness, helmet, prusiks, and crampons and rope up with Tim, Merle and Scott and to the summit from 15,200 to 17,200. Long, slow and tough. Many thoughts, but mostly total focus on where to put the next step, always looking for a crevasse."

You can climb alone and not come back, or climb in teams. We climbed in teams of four and crossed and climbed ice, snow, and rock roped together in a line. Each climber had to stay about 25 feet behind the one in front and keep the rope loose but somewhat taut. If a climber slipped over the side or fell into a crevasse, the other three would help pull him out. That's what they told me. The leader sets the pace, and the pace always seemed to be like horses racing. No, a team leader understands that a team progresses according to the slowest member. And the slowest member soon realizes it's necessary to reach back for a little extra, which is tough to do when there is little extra back there. I hung in there. What was I going to do, take my ice axe and go home?

If you begin to slide or fall, another safety measure is to strike the point of your ice ax into the ice above you to stop sliding and falling. This maneuver can prevent a "thud" echoing up the mountain after however long it takes to plummet through the air to a soft grassy spot 3,000 feet below. An ice ax also serves as a cane or crutch in snow and ice like some of us older people use to climb stairs.

I am frequently asked, "Were you scared?" Yes, I was, but Linus has his security blanket and I was hooked to a rope. It's scary going it alone in any life endeavor. In awesome settings, there is the tendency to take it all in, gawk and gaze with every step. One must remain calm and focused in precarious situations. Even during treks and hikes in most higher and steeper places, it's vital to continue looking down with every step. Otherwise, you might stumble over a rock and break a leg or fall into a place that will cost your family an evacuation fee. The rate is the same, dead or alive. When climbing, the total focus is on the next step and the next gasp of thin air to fuel the next step. It's total concentration on looking where the next step is placed. Stop and then look up at the summit. In measuring the distance to a summit, 100 feet appears to be a mile. From my journal:

"At about 12 noon, the base of the summit, a steep rocky point about 12 feet across. Two fixed ropes set by Dimitri and Juan for us to clip onto and rock climb up 15 feet to the next level and then the summit. All made it and Tim firmly shook my hand offering, "Congratulations." Others also congratulated me, mentioning my birthday. Photos and a joyous celebration."

The summit of Pyramide Blanca is a flat rock, a bit larger than a kitchen table. I sat down and looked around and down. When I say down, I mean way down. What a sight! I'd never had such feelings, emotions, and sensations, surprise and disbelief all crammed together in a flurry of thoughts. And then a peacefully joyous pause transformed the moment to a settled calm. But while clinging to the rocky summit, the whirlwind of thoughts and questions persisted. Where am I? Why did I come here? What force intervened, providing the strength? My silent response and acknowledgement was simple and brief. "I'm richly blessed."

When asked weeks later how I felt at the summit, my response was spontaneous. "I felt closer to God."

There is the thrill of victory and the agony of getting there. But victory is incomplete until you are cuddling in the sleeping bag back at camp. What goes up must come down. Oh, Lord, help me! From my journal:

"Clip back onto two fixed ropes and down the two rocky slopes. Very, very hard on legs and knees and more dangerous than ascending. At one point, we had to rappel down a cliff and then cross a wide crevasse and ice cave. Four p.m. and exhausted with two miles down to camp. So exhausted, but elated. Had not stopped since 4:30 a.m. The few rest stops were of little relief. Totally spent and wobbled back to camp. Such emotional thoughts, but again focused on making it to camp. Staggered to dining tent and a bit of tea. Since 5 a.m., had only one candy bar, one liter of water and one liter of Gatorade. Cate gave me a half-liter going back to camp. Dinner at 6:30. Brendan and Tim went to cooking tent and brought in a birthday cake molded from chocolate bars with one lit candle on top. (Cate and Brendan had actually planned to have the cake on the summit, but forgot and left it in a pack at the base.) Totally exhausted, but filled with emotional energy. Sleep by 9:00. What a memorable birthday!"

The following day was a rest day, if washing a few clothes in an icy stream and practicing crevasse rescue is considered restful. We spent the day preparing for the next day's climb. From my journal:

"Arose at 4:00, dry cereal. Put on boots, gear and headlamp and two miles to the glacier. Difficult. Hiking up and over rocks with a heavy pack in darkness using a headlamp is like riding a bicycle blindfolded up Pike's Peak. Daybreak at 6:30. Put on gear and up glacier. Did OK to first summit, then down rocky slope and over icy-razor ridge. Steep ice climb to the next summit. Didn't have the strength, energy or will to attack it. Juan roped me to a large rock and I sat for an hour or so watching the team make summit. Stayed fairly warm in 30-mile wind. Back up the rocky point and over glacier, two miles to camp. Exhausted."

OK, so I chickened out. A dead chicken lays no eggs, but there was another fish to fry. The next day, we packed up camp, loaded the gear on the llamas, which the farmer had brought back to carry the gear to the waiting bus and rode to the next mountain. My notes revealed one small pleasure in life, "Good to sit on a seat."

Huayana Potosi is 20,000 feet high, and what a beautiful, but imposing sight from the valley. In two days, I'd be on the top. The next morning, we broke camp at the valley at 15,000 feet and began the two-day, five thousand foot climb. From my journal:

"Loaded up gear for high camp at about 17,000 feet. Carried camera, candy bars, down jacket, extra fleece and polypro, sleeping bag, part of tent, crampons, ice axe, helmet, harness, carbiners, prusiks, and two liters of water, a bowl, spoon and cup. Must have weighed 50 pounds. Wore heavy climbing boots. Very arduous climb, one of the most physically demanding things I've ever done. Set up high camp on steep rocky point and tent on flat rocks. Large boulders separated tents and had to scramble to maneuver. Milled about resting in the sun rest of afternoon. Shared tent with Colin from Tasmania. Sleeping bag had not been satisfactory during cold nights. Always piled down coat and jackets on bag at night. Slept in polypro and fleece and three pair wool socks. Dinner of hot noodles at 6:00 and in sleeping bag at 7:30. Tomorrow climb Huayana Potosi.

Hot tea and oatmeal at 3:30 from Francisco as always. Then scramble in crowded tent to dress and pack for climb. Had not slept well as wind beat against tent wall at 40 miles per hour during the night and was apprehensive about the climb. Had to unzip the tent five times during the night and go out to urinate. Stars were awesome. Had used bottle to urinate prior, but with Colin sharing tent, decided not to take the bottle. Roped up with Juan leading, Merle, Dimitri and me. Began the roped train up steep part of glacier with headlamps at 4:15. Still apprehensive about my strength and will. Could always stop and use my age as the reason since the other 11-team members are all under 38."

When climbing, the focus is always on the next step. You don't think of your age, the weather, your physical or mental condition or anything else. The total focus is on the next step. The next step could take you into a crevasse, over a several-thousand-foot drop, or if you're on loose rocks or gravel, down a steep slope. The only other focus is on breathing. I kept up as our train proceeded very slowly.

My thoughts had shifted from apprehension and uncertainty to the next step, keeping the rope always on the downside and the ice axe on the upside. We climbed in darkness and in silence. The sky began to lighten at 6:30 and then the sun peeked over the mountain. In high altitudes, as soon as the sun strikes you, it is like moving closer to a warm stove. Brendan said it would be a six-hour climb to the base of the summit. If it's too grueling, can't I take my ice axe and go back to my tent home? I could if I knew how to get back.

We came to a 150-foot icefall. Brendan, Tim and Juan free climbed to set fixed ropes. I'd had brief instruction and a bit of experience on the previous climb on 60-80 degree ice. You kick the two front points of the crampons (ten points on the bottom) firmly into the ice and remain balanced with most of the pressure on the calf muscles. Then you strike the ice axe—sometimes 3-4 attempts—until the point "thuds" and is firmly implanted in the ice, pull up, make other toeholds and keep going until you get to the top. It's quite exhausting, but climbers love it. After reaching the base of the summit, about 500 yards away, we dropped our packs and carried only cameras and water. I was exhausted and thought of waiting there. Why go on, but then why not? When I thought I couldn't go another step, a mysterious force once again injected me with a boost of energy.

Thanks, I needed that. With the summit within range, our three teams went to work; no stopping us now.

We're there! We can look down now, and what a sight! From the top of Huayana Potosi, the view is spectacular. It's true, on a clear day you can see forever. I had attained my two goals; making it to the top and climbing to 20,000 feet. It was party time, a time to congratulate all other team members and a time to shout it out—unrestrained joy and exhilaration. It was also a time to reflect upon the serenity and the majesty of the surrounding landscape, a vast space packed with miles and miles of snowy peaks—all below us. From that perspective, it was surreal, like a mystical and enchanting dream in another world formed in fantasy.

With elation and satisfaction, we roped up and started down. The sun reflected brilliantly off the ice and snow. The cloud I was on would gently lower me to the bottom, right? No, it would not, but my legs and knees would. If maneuvering over rocks, one must determine if the rocks are stationary or loose. If on packed snow and ice, each step with the crampons must be firmly embedded in the ice. The weight of the pack and body naturally pushes down and the legs and knees serve as a braking mechanism, requiring them to be in a bent or stooped position. Slowly and methodically, we crept to the dreaded icefall. It was like looking down from the top of a ten-story building and seeing jagged ice covering the sidewalk. Attached to fixed ropes at the top, each of us individually took our turn. Being an old climbing pro after three weeks, I felt more confident. It was difficult and scary, but I landed on the bottom, and thanked God that my life had not ended with a thud.

When we got down to the high camp at the ledge of large boulders, we packed up the remaining gear and tents. It was around 2:00 p.m. and I'd had no food since the bowl of oatmeal at 3:30 a.m. except two power bars, a liter of iodine water and a liter of Gatorade. I was spent, but had to take the heavy pack down to the valley. Slush, loose rock and steep grades required utmost caution and consumed nearly two hours and my final reserve of energy. When I reached the valley with a half-mile to the spot where we were to be picked up by bus, I was totally exhausted and had to struggle to maintain balance. Finally, I made it back to base camp where peanut butter snacks and fruit reinforced me during the brief wait for the 90-minute ride back to La Paz.

When we arrived at the hotel, I struggled to carry my two stuffed duffle bags and crammed backpack up the steps to my room. I dumped the filthy clothes all over the room to dry and air out. I hadn't showered for days, and only had one brief upper-body wash in an icy stream and limited use of baby wipes. I hadn't changed my underwear and climbing apparel for about a week. It's amazing how a long hot shower comforts, relaxes and refreshes.

"Hey guys, let's go out and have a salad and some pizza and down it with a beer or two." Does it get any better than this?

It's 10:00 p.m., and I have a clean body, clean clothes, clean sheets, a nice warm bed and a full stomach. What a day! What a 19-hour day! What a remarkable and grand day!

A year and a half later, my blood began boiling again. Why don't you cool it? OK, I'll go to Ecuador. I've heard the mountains there are beautiful and the summits provide extraordinary views. My family tossed in the towel. Once it gets in his head, you can't convince him otherwise. This time, it has to be the onset of dementia.

My retirement had developed into a routine of undertaking at least one big challenge each year. Plan it, work toward it, train for it and do it. Trek, climb or run a marathon this year and do another adventurous and exciting thing next year. When the extreme physical challenges became somewhat less demanding, I put my brain to work, what a shocker, and began writing a book nearly every year. Climbing and running are physically difficult; writing articles and books requires less oxygen, but the mental effort is like running your brain through a torture chamber. Who said retirement would be easy? After my first climbing adventure in Bolivia in 1999, I ran the New York Marathon the next year. Then the "what's next" bug began to bite again. I contacted my friend Cate, who had been on our climbs in Bolivia, and, prior to that, had climbed in Ecuador.

"Cate, can I do it?"

"Yes, you can."

I contacted the American Alpine Institute and signed up for a climbing expedition in Ecuador. My buddy, young, highly competent and skilled Brendan, who was our guide in Bolivia, had been assigned as the guide for the expedition in Ecuador. Familiarity breeds contempt, but in this case, it bred confidence. Then I was flooded with information about travel and reservations, immunizations, climbing equipment, clothing, medicine, etc., and an evacuation insurance policy application. If I'm on the side of a mountain and break a leg, crack my head or become delirious, a helicopter will pick me up, if there's a place to land it.

Ecuador is a beautiful country, mountainous with adjacent rolling hills covered with lush green vegetation. The climate is perfect for growing roses, which are exported daily to the United States. Fresh roses from Ecuador are preferable to the assortment of plastic ones from the Far East. A country's landscape dotted with roses is an open invitation to its beauty. Quito, the capital, is clean, orderly and quite impressive, sitting amidst lush, green rolling hills, which taper down into scenic little valleys below.

One of the first chores when entering a strange country is converting dollars into the local currency. I could never keep those calculations in my head. At the time, the money conversion problem in Ecuador was that a dollar equaled 25 thousand sucre. If a sandwich cost 20,000 sucre, it set you back 80 cents. When our team of 11 assembled the first day, we went out to dinner and equally split the bill. It took Brenden at least a half hour to count out the sucres, and the stack of bills reached about five inches high.

As usual, our team was a great bunch of guys with no gals this time. The eleven members included a couple of Wall Street bond traders, a scientist for a pharmaceutical company and a "music" lawyer. Mark was a young hippy-haired lawyer who did legal and contractual work for some well-known musicians. A year earlier, he had helped arrange a music festival exchange between the U.S. and Cuba. Mark was the kind of guy who could talk his way into the gold vault at Fort Knox. When he went to Cuba to work out the arrangements for the festival, he told an official he wanted Fidel Castro to sign a baseball for him. Mark was a baseball fan and collected baseballs signed by not only famous players, but other noted celebrities. Later, the Cuban official sent Mark to Fidel's office and they chatted about music and baseball. Perhaps as a gesture of goodwill, Fidel signed two baseballs for him.

Mark later called Ronald Reagan's office and requested another baseball signing. It was during the president's waning days as his illness had progressed to its latter stages. Mark was given an appointment, perhaps one of the last the former president conducted. They chatted and the president told him about his experiences in office, and signed the baseball.

Mark and I began to pal around and often hiked and climbed together. I liked hearing his stories, and he picked my brain, knowing I had spent a lifetime trying to educate, rehabilitate and co-exist with America's youth. He had a six-year-old son whom he loved more than rock music or baseball. He was deeply concerned about raising his son the right way, but was apprehensive about the modern youth culture boiling within an unstable and uncertain society. I avoided relating too many horror stories and explained that his sincere love and concern indicated his son would turn out well, although the pain, at times, would seem unbearable. I warned him that in a few short years, his son would begin to shun and dislike him, but not to worry because his allegiance had shifted to his crazy mixed-up peers. I also cautioned him that when his son began combing his hair without nagging, girls had entered his life, causing him to lose interest in school and devote his life to becoming a rock musician, which seemed to him the quickest way to attract groupies of the opposite sex. And this too shall pass, and your son will likely become a whiz in the computer field or find a home on Wall Street. So are the conversations on a mountain when there's little else to do, except gasp for breath.

What is the first thing you do when you're on site preparing for a climb? You got it—acclimatize and practice. We drove two hours from Quito for the next three days and hiked in the mountains. On the last day of preparation, we hiked 15,000 feet over uneven lava rock up to a volcano. The problem with volcanoes is they erupt. One had blown a few days earlier near where we were. The air was somewhat ashy. Can one run away from molten lava?

My last day of preparation was the pits, as in a toilet. It was one of those days when your stomach ingested something and then rejected it, like a motor rejects water in the tank. It belches, sputters and spews. Where's a porta-potty when you need one?

In most all travels abroad, the stomach is one of your more precious possessions. If it sours, churns, or is poisoned, the last thing you feel like doing is hiking in high altitudes. An upset stomach dehydrates and weakens the body. Climbing requires hydration and strength. On all my excursions, usually a few or all members of the group contracted diarrhea at some point along the way. However, in all cases, we eventually overcame the alarming malady. Despite my weakened condition, my stomach began cooperating, and I made it through the day.

The next day, we loaded up and headed for the base of Cayambe, a 19,000-foot peak. A crude hut had been erected there for climbers to use, eliminating the need for tents. We spent the day practicing on the glacier in low-cast weather, which blocked the view of Cayambe hovering directly above us. Early the next morning, I walked outside the hut under a beautifully, clear, blue sky. There it was! The majestic mountain protruding up and over me, covered with layered capes of pure-white snow. I'm standing down here looking up. Tonight, I'll climb up there. The view from down here is awesome. What will be the word to describe the view from up there?

When I said, "climb tonight" that's what I meant. Brenden instructed us that dinner would be at 7:00, hit the bed at 8:00, awakened at 11:30 for breakfast at 12:00 midnight and begin climbing at 12:30. He also told us that if we couldn't sleep, to lie still, stay calm and close our eyes because we'd need every ounce of energy we could store.

If you knew your first child would be born at 12:30 a.m., could you go to sleep three hours prior? If you faced execution at daybreak and your last meal was oatmeal, could you go to sleep hoping you'd die peacefully before they turned on the juice? I tossed and turned until the midnight breakfast, which was at the time I'd usually have my compulsory midnight snack in preparation to snuggle warmly and dream pleasant dreams about exotic foods and sunny beaches.

Without sleep, I wobbled out of the hut into utter darkness and a snowstorm. Turning on my headlamp, all I could see were big, fat, white flakes floating lazily to the earth. After one hour of going up a steep rocky slope, we roped up and I followed the moving object in front of me who was hooked, I hoped to the same rope tied to me. This nonsense went on for hours. From my journal:

"Could not sleep. Up at 11:30, climb at 12:30. Started up difficult steep rocky slope in snowy weather. After one hour, put on crampons, ropes, etc., which is always fun. After team ready, Mark had to go to bathroom in snow. Up the mountain slow and steady as snow kept falling. Without any sleep, I felt very tired, but had to find strength to climb. Time passed rather quickly and the moon broke through the snowy clouds and gave enough light to climb without the headlamps. Wove up through beautiful, blue ice craters. Finally, daylight and the summit in sight. Tired, but kept moving. To summit, one always wants to stop, but you keep going. Jim, Bob, Mark, Craig and I made it at 9:30 a.m. The summit was a rounded dome covered with packed snow and large enough for 6-8 guys to stand. The sky was partially clear and the wind blew at 40 mph. Magnificent and stunning! After about 10 minutes of photos and congratulations, we started the difficult descent. My legs soon began feeling the pressure and the pounding. My right leg gave way on two occasions from sheer exhaustion and I fell on the snow and ice. At about 10:30 the snow began softening, which clogs the crampons and makes descending nearly impossible. Jim taped ripped plastic bags to our feet and it worked. At 12:30 we arrived at the base of the glacier. One-half hour down the rocky slope and to the hut at 1:00 p.m. for soup and grilled-cheese sandwiches. To bed at 2:00 and sleep until 4:00. Up for dinner and then a good night's sleep. Talked to Brenden about going back home due to my legs not being up to it. Wait until tomorrow to decide or he can arrange for me to go back after the climb at Cotopaxi."

OK, so I chickened out again. I had my first knee operation 10 months prior to Cayambe. I'd been apprehensive about the trip and possible further damage to my knees. Although running was not a problem, climbing was a different matter because of the consistent and continuous stress, strain and pounding on the legs. The day after Cayambe, my 65-year-old legs felt like they might drop off. What if they had to carry me to the plane? Brendan arranged for me to return to Quito, and I flew to Miami and home two days later.

If I had it to do over, I would probably continue with the group. But perhaps it was just as well, because they went on to climb Cotopaxi, but had to turn back 500 feet from the summit because of the danger of an avalanche. That would have been exciting. And a severe storm prevented the group from attempting Chimborazo. My primary concern was that I might do permanent damage to my legs and knees. So why did I go? A doctor friend once told me. "Enjoy life and do what you want to do, and if you need a knee replacement, so what?" When I heard the Dalai Lama give a talk to thousands in a basketball arena, his first statement was, "I believe we're on this earth to be happy." His fans stood and cheered. With those bits of advice, I decided to roll on. I had heard you only go around once, but I wanted to disprove that theory because retirement provides the chance to go around twice.

Bad knees or not, three years later, I trekked to above base camp at K2, the second tallest mountain in the world. Four years after that, I attempted to climb Aconcaqua in Argentina, the tallest mountain in the Western Hemisphere.

Retirement is a blast. When your rocket ship returns to earth after one flight, light the fuse for another adventure, and always keep your matches dry.

CHAPTER 8

YOU MIGHT BE A GOD

❖ ❖ ❖

After planting a seed, I try to move on before the grass begins growing under my feet. Hanging around the house is mowing the lawn and painting the walls with a softer tint.

To avoid stir craziness, I fastened my seatbelt again and began another jaunt halfway around the world. This trip was significantly different from my others in that I'd be staying in homes with families. During one of the first home stays, the gentleman informed me, "You might be a god, so we'll treat you like one." I don't think I meet the qualifications and am convinced I'm not one unless everyone is. I should have announced to my host that many years prior, I'd been rejected in my quest to attain the status of becoming anything God-like. My month-long trip to India was unlike any other. How does one treat a god visiting your home?

Staying in hotels or tents, one can tour and see the physical aspects of a country or area. Living in homes with the people, particularly those of a much different culture, provides a clearer understanding and insight into how diverse people actually experience life. Guests are usually treated hospitably in our country, but we seldom shower them with adoration.

Having been a member of a Rotary Club for several years, I was selected to lead a Group Study Exchange team from Rotary International's District 6580, consisting of 32 clubs in southern Indiana, to District 3090 in Punjab, which is located in the northern part of India bordering Pakistan, Kashmir and China.

Rotary International is a service organization with over 1,234,000 members dispersed in 33,790 clubs throughout the world. The Rotary motto is, "Service Above Self." All local Rotary Clubs conduct service projects for their respective communities, and Rotary International sponsors humanitarian projects throughout the world including health, clean water, sanitation, hunger relief and literacy.

In 1985, Rotary International undertook a massive project to eradicate polio throughout the world. The initial goal of the Polio Plus project was to raise $120 million. To indicate the extent of commitment and service, local Rotary clubs raised $240 million. Since the initial undertaking, Rotary has raised over $800 million to eradicate the dreaded, crippling disease. Over two billion children have been immunized at a cost of 60 cents per dose. Although most parts of the world are now polio free, there are cases remaining in four under-developed countries. The project will continue until every child in the world is immunized. I'm proud and pleased to have been a very small part of this most worthy endeavor.

To promote world peace and understanding, Rotary International sponsors many Group Study

Exchange programs each year. A Rotary district, composed of around 30 clubs, selects a team to exchange with a district from another part of the world. The team leader is required to be a Rotarian, but the other four members of the team cannot be a member or directly related to a Rotarian. One other requirement is that team members must be under the age of 45. A team is composed of people representing diverse professions and businesses. Costs include only the passport and immunization fees. Rotary International provides airfare, and after the hosts meet the team at the airport, all food, lodging and entertainment is provided. You might check with your local Rotary Club if you are longing to take a cost-free trip to another part of the world. These group-study-exchange tours are excellent opportunities.

Late one cold winter evening, on January 30, 1994, Phyllis, a nurse, Karleen, a clinical psychologist, Tom, an industrial supervisor, Steve, a county judge and I flew from Louisville to Cincinnati to Frankfurt to New Delhi. After a gracious welcome at the airport, our hosts loaded our weary team in vehicles for a three-hour drive to Rajpura.

In the U.S., traffic is bad day and night. At 12:00 midnight in New Delhi, the streets were deserted, but our cars had to keep stopping. Sacred cows were out roaming most everywhere. Welcome to a month of culture shock.

After the 28-hour journey and finally to bed, we were awakened four hours later to begin promoting peace and good will. An elementary school was our first stop. Upon arrival, we were seated at the front of the rows of chairs in the schoolyard. The children, dressed in attractive uniforms, marched out in an orderly and precise manner to drum beats, and took their seats. Even the little six-year olds sat through the hour-long program with undivided attention. Impressive! Try that at the Happy Trail Elementary School in your neighborhood.

The first order of business was a garland ceremony. Five students were designated to garland us, placing a string of flowers around our necks. We were garlanded two or three times each day. A gift of beautiful flowers was symbolic of the extraordinary welcome and hospitality afforded us throughout our visit to that fascinating country.

Principal Pal (pronounced Paul) gave the welcome and then asked the children, teachers and guests to rise and sing the India national anthem. The bright sunrays were blinding. My road map, bloodshot eyes begged for relief as my body and mind lagged 12 hours behind me. My team was in a similar shape, or worse. Principal Pal then announced, "Our American guests will now sing their national anthem, The Star Spangled Banner." Do what? I've joined in singing our anthem thousands of times, but can't ever remember getting all the way through it, particularly the "o'er the land of the free" part.

I'm the leader with a quick decision to make. Do I make an excuse—we're jet lagged out of our skulls, we haven't practiced, we forgot the words. I stood up and motioned for our team to stand, praying that at least one team member could sing. The rest of us could perhaps lip sync it through. We were like zombies in a strange land, standing before an audience of inquisitive children, teachers and guests. A team leader must be prepared to face any crisis. In battle, fire the first shot. Clearing my scratchy throat, "Oh, say can you (finish this song?), and the home of the brave." Perhaps it was the Hindu God of Courage who carried us through.

From that first visit to the school on the early morning of our first day in India, we toured a cotton mill, a margarine and bicycle factories and a plant that manufactured large steel cables. After the long flight, little sleep and embarrassment singing our national anthem, I lost consciousness when they began eagerly showing us how to make margarine.

During that month, our team visited 15 different Rotary clubs in 15 towns and small cities in Punjab. We usually stayed in different homes for one or two nights, and then moved on to the next host club in another town.

From that initial stop over and gracious welcome, we visited 68 other schools, universities, factories, hospitals, museums, forts, temples, farms, banks, government offices and were entertained daily with speeches, music, folk dancing and food, food and more food. Some of the food was a mystery, most of it was spicy, and the large amounts forced down our throats challenged the physical laws restricting expansion of the intestinal tract. Whatever your image of God, he/she is undoubtedly overweight.

Most Americans eat two quick meals each day and get nourishment from snacking hourly during a 24-hour cycle. How does one adjust to five meals per day, by vomiting at least twice each day? No, you work out a plan. Here is how I organized our five meals per day itinerary.

It became apparent early on that the people in these outer environs wanted to see, meet and touch their guests. It was as if, we've heard many stories about Americans, but we want to understand what they are really like? Above all, we want to make an impression by revealing our generous hospitality, and the best way to warm their hearts is to feed them a continuous flow of spicy things. Spicy things do warm the body to the degree you think certain parts might ignite.

Often, there would be 15 to 25 neighbors and friends at a lavish early-morning breakfast. Then at mid-morning, the caravan would leave for a tour of a factory (we toured five cotton mills), hospital, school, palace or another institution and a friendly welcome, which included another banquet table. After observing the process of how cotton becomes t-shirts, it was time for several speeches and a huge lunch. In the afternoon, two more welcome ceremonies at two more factories, schools or shrines, and two more tables loaded with food.

We can't keep on doing this. They haven't given us time for the jet lag to clear. We don't want our seething, spewing insides causing an international incident. Where can we get another shipment of Pepto-Bismol?

After another exhaustive, jam-packed day, we'd be taken back to our host's home to rest for what seemed like 15 minutes before being transported to another banquet hall to party with a large group of community notables.

To party in American is to talk, laugh, eat and drink, some of which will cause a tipsy condition. It's the same in India. The women frequently separate from the men in another room or area to talk and eat. The men assemble where the bottles are and drink, talk, laugh and eat dainty, spicy things before re-gathering for the main meal. In India, they distill and generously serve a brand of Scotch called Peter Scot and a popular brewed beer known as Thunderbolt. It is. One evening as the party continued, I looked at my watch, and it was past midnight. "Oh, come on now, I'll pile up another plate of food for you." No, thanks, I've had enough Thunderbolt and your thunderbolt food for one evening.

We can't go on like this. They've worn us down. We're on the go and never have any private time. They all seem to want a piece of us. The food thing is killing us. They take us by the arm to a table and practically force us to take another plate of food. What do we do, refuse and become more ugly Americans?

A leader must think and be decisive when encountering any crisis. Although it was logistically difficult to conduct a secret meeting, I gathered my team together to plot strategy. I reminded them we were on a mission to promote good will and that, when in the center of a mob around a table, we should always hold a plate of food in our hand. I sensed the team thought I'd totally lost it, but I explained how my cleverly designed plan would not only promote good will, but also prevent us from throwing up so much.

My strategy was to take a plate of food, a little bit of this and a little bit of that, then walk around taking tiny bites every few minutes. Continue chewing whether there is food in your mouth or not. Then glance around and set the plate down where no one will notice. Wander off until another Indian takes you by the arm and to the table. Continue repeating this procedure throughout the evening. One of the four guidelines Rotarians try to live by is, "Is it the truth?" Yes, my excess food intake plan was the truth.

The Punjab area is primarily a flat and level land and had been an arid wasteland until an irrigation system was developed. The melting waters of the Himalayas flowing down from the north transformed an unproductive area into a fertile and productive one. Excellent fruits, vegetables and grains are grown in the vast rural area. The citrus was the sweetest I've ever eaten. The vegetables were well formed and delicious. Radishes grew to six inches in length. In the 1960's, the introduction of a special type of wheat to the fertile area was a lifesaver and a miracle.

Norman Borlaug, an American, is recognized as having done more to alleviate world hunger than any other individual. Experimenting in genetically engineered foods, he developed a type of Mexican wheat, of which the yield in India doubled in a very short time. India has a high rate of poverty as evidenced on our tour. However, hunger and starvation is not a critical problem due primarily to the advancements in agricultural production, particularly the abundance of wheat. In highly productive years, India exports wheat to other countries.

If God came to your home, would you ignore him? Of course not. First, you'd make certain he was well fed. If he were hungry, he might become irritable. You'd also be eager to show him around and want all your friends to come and gawk at him. You'd never want him to be alone, because he might think you lacked interest in the afterlife. I can understand why God avoids leaving heaven's premises, preferring to remain there where it is always peaceful and the pace is not like rats racing to a garbage dump.

I'm just a common, ordinary guy, not a president of anything, except my Rotary Club once, and I'm not a member of President Clinton's cabinet. However, if I'm one of the many Hindu gods, I wish I'd known. Every day I gave several speeches and talks, posed endlessly for photographs and signed autographs until my hand cramped. Our hosts insisted our team take part in all kinds of events. Name a ceremony and we were involved, except funerals and the reincarnation process. On one occasion, when I got out of the car at a girls' school, they mobbed me and practically knocked me to the ground. My hosts had to rescue me. Now I have a vague idea what Elvis endured.

From the time the plane touched down in Delhi, the initial culture shock and the subsequent month of action-packed activity overwhelmed us. It was like preparing for a race, and on the first training day, the coach had you run a marathon. After a couple of days, our team began feeling as if we had involuntarily signed up for a type of rigorous boot camp. March over hill, chow down; march over dale, chow down. I suggested we be patient, and just go with the flow, which is tough if you're going over Niagara Falls. We did adjust somewhat and learned to go with the flow, plunged into a churning sea of humanity.

Americans want to live independently and demand considerable amounts of privacy. You can get lost in a crowd, but not in India. It seemed when we did have a few hours to barricade ourselves in a bedroom, people were outside the door listening to us snore. When short "rest" periods were set aside, it meant time to sit down, eat, talk and respond to questions about what America is really like, which is literally indescribable.

Two questions kept popping up. Why do more than half of our marriages end in divorce, and why do we place our old folks in places called rest homes? Perhaps we should consider arranging our marriages like they do. One father told me dating was prohibited. A young man could never call on his daughter and be alone with her in the same room. Their system of arranged marriages seems to work, because divorce is rare. If I had it to do over, I would have handpicked my daughter's husband.

A culture that takes personal care of their elderly is an admirable trait worthy of consideration, but we don't have the time, do we? Our system is based upon providing financial security for our elderly so they can live out the latter years without being a burden to their children. If they become unable to live alone, we place them in another home to rest.

During my two or three day visits with several different families primarily in middle and upper-middle-class homes, without exception, the occupants of a home not only included the father, mother and children, but one, two, three or more older grandparents, uncles, aunts and others. Trying to answer the question as best I could, I explained that both husband and wife need to work to make financial ends meet, we're very busy and our elderly enjoy living with their peers. My explanation usually bounced off blank stares.

I also asked a few questions. When in Sirsa with Raghavendra Rao, a very bright, 34 year-old who was a government commissioner essentially in charge of over one million people, I asked if he had problems with juvenile delinquency. He said, "No."

None? "Not really." Now do I have this right? They keep the extended family together, divorce is rare and their kids don't run the streets.

During my long life in the United States, I've participated in two marriage ceremonies; my own, which my wife arranged, and my only daughter's marriage 30 years later. "Here comes the bride, here comes the bride—and her giddy, goofy dad."

In my month in India, I participated in two wedding ceremonies, one a wedding reception and the other a group wedding. There must have been a thousand guests under a huge tent celebrating the marriage of a young couple with music, young native dancers and food and more food. When we Americans crashed it, they escorted me up to the platform to join the bride and groom. I am shy and didn't want to be put on that spot. What would I do? You'll stand there, greet the guests and be photographed with the newly married couple a hundred times. Remember, you're doing this for your country.

Then the rains came. A scattered shower here is a monsoon there. Circus-sized tents are not designed to withstand hurricanes and the amount of water Noah encountered when gathering all the animals. The reception ended before its time, after every guest had their fancy clothes thoroughly washed and each human body had all the impurities cleansed from every pore. What a night!

The next day, more tours to cotton mills, schools or a place where bricks are baked. Thanking them for another warm or hot experience, particularly if it's a brickyard, is the protocol. And always add, "Isn't this fascinating?" It was interesting and particularly humbling to see these simple folk devoted to their work. Their warm smiles in return revealing appreciation, were gratifying and inspiring. Ghandi talked about the nobility of manual labor. These people performed their work in that fashion.

On this particular day, we travelled to another large tent filled with people from the surrounding villages. Just as the group wedding (10 couples) was about to begin, I was escorted down an aisle crowded with villagers who were sitting on the ground. My Rotarian host seated me on the ground beside a Sikh clergyman. All eyes were focused on my grand entrance. Why did he put me in this very conspicuous spot? Apparently, the 10 couples would consider it an honor for an American "leader" to take part in their group wedding. I plopped down and crossed my legs, attempting to sit like the Sikh clergyman. Before the ceremony ended, I'd developed severe leg cramps.

Seventy percent of the one billion people in India live in rural villages. One host told me that many people in these villages had never seen an American. Thus, our welcome and receptions in the villages were extraordinarily special. At one village, our grand entry was by camel back. As we raced through the streets, hundreds of excited villagers eagerly followed shouting and laughing.

Of all our visits in Punjab, the ones to the villages were the most impressive and memorable. Poverty was obvious, but there was an undercurrent of a simplistic richness and spiritual abundance. We saw men sitting under trees in the evenings learning how to read. We saw women drawing water at the only village well. We saw humility amidst what could be termed hopelessness, but when that vital spirit for life remains deeply at the core, the beauty and dignity of every life should somehow be allowed to shine, as does the life-sustaining sun.

At the village of Kaimire, some of the women demonstrated how they were learning to sew on (new to them) used sewing machines. The women were eager, proud and pleased to show us their work. When the Rotarian host informed me that his club in Hirsa was raising money to buy used sewing machines for the village, I told him I would present the project to my club, and perhaps we could help. Upon returning to my club, I showed my video of the village. Our team and club raised $4,000 to purchase used sewing machines for the village of Kaimire.

There I was, seated beside the Sikh. What did they expect me to do, announce, "I now pronounce you man and wife," 10 times? I don't speak a Hindi dialect or any dialect other than a combination of a Midwestern and Southern drawl. Nothing else to do but sit, so I turned my video camera on and filmed each of the beautiful young couples as they walked up the crowded aisle to take their brief vows. Perhaps I wasn't so special. Every wedding needs an official photographer. Do I ever have a real treasure on film!

Each day presented new and different experiences. The cotton mills got a bit dull, but most of our overnight stays in different homes became a kind of, "We'll outdo the Joneses." Since most Rotarians in India are professionals, landowners or in business, some of the homes we visited bordered on the ones lining our "Million Dollar Rows." However, the amenities and conveniences are not what we have. In one very fine home, the wife was eager to have her servants do our laundry. She explained our clothes would not be hung on a line outside to dry, because, finally, she had a new electric clothes dryer. We stayed with a medical doctor behind the walls of a compound guarded by the military. He was on a hit list and a target from terrorists in nearby Pakistan. I did not ask why. No matter the affluence of a particular family, our welcome was always extravagant. In the middle-class homes, the toilet was a hole in a tile floor, and the shower was a bucket of warm water. When simple folks honor your presence, the moments are ones to cherish.

One of my more memorable visits was in Sirsa with Rao Raghavendra and his family. He was a bright, young Deputy Commissioner who governed over one million people. He and his family lived in a compound consisting of a 19th century British manor surrounded by beautiful gardens. When touring the area, Rao and I sat in the back seat of his chauffer-driven sedan, trailed by a fleet of military vehicles. I'm not a representative of our State Department, but a former down-to-earth dirt farmer, teacher and school administrator swamped with kids most of my life. Maybe I am more important than I think I am, because when Rao and I would get out of the car, after the chauffer opened the door, the people would make way for us and some would even bow to the commissioner and me. Stuff gets in your head when you're treated like royalty. Rao gave me the treatment. When I bid farewell, he said, "Your visit will be unforgettable." And so is he.

"We have no system." That is how a host explained traffic in India. My notes verify their lack of a traffic system, which requires constant prayer to the God of Narrow Escapes:

"People, bicycles, scooters, rickshaws, three-wheel taxis, three-wheel trucks, big Tata trucks and beat-up buses packed with people on the top and hanging on were everywhere. Carts pulled by donkeys, small horses, water buffalo, Brahmin bulls, camels, and tractors pulling wagons were everywhere. People packed on streets, beautifully clothed women with large baskets of dung, grass or twigs piled on their head, two-wheel carts hauling everything. Many narrow escapes. Satish (our driver) was skilled, but drove too fast through towns, weaving in and out missing bicycles (crashing into only one) and people by inches. On the open road, he played the bluffing game, getting within inches when passing big trucks and buses or meeting them head on until one took a ditch."

I sat beside Satish every day and kept my video camera on the dash, ready for the unexpected, but you can expect most anything on the roads in India. Don't hit the camel or the herd of cows; they have the right of way. Miss that load of hay. Why is that elephant in the road? The bus barreling down the road will hit us unless you take the ditch. Satish drove up to one cow practically nudging it with the bumper. She wouldn't move until she was finished using the rest-stop bathroom in the middle of the road. Of all the films of my adventures I show to groups, the segment on "we have no system" creates the greatest response. It's one, "Oh, no," after the other.

With our lives intact, one last event remained before leaving the buzzing and swarming beehive. It must have been a political rally of some sort. We were escorted to a large courtyard where hundreds of people were seated under a bright morning sun. After music and several shorter speeches, a big-shot official of some sort took the podium and kept it, rambling on and on in a dialect. The blazing sun blending with his fiery pleas began to rub a nerve or two. Remember to be patient, but won't you please shut up. Dazed and semi-conscious, I suddenly jerked up when I heard five words in English, "Terry Coomins (his pronunciation) and Bill Clinton." A bit later, "Terry Coomins and Bill Clinton." Bill Clinton doesn't know me. Armed guards surrounded us with fixed guns. He said it a third time, forcefully and with emotion. I sat up straighter listening intently. Was he praising the president and me, or was it a hostile tirade? If pressed, I'll tell them I voted Republican.

It would require more chapters to give a complete account of our team's 30 days in India. In reviewing my journal and notes, these phrases kept popping up—unbelievable, an awesome experience, they did not want us to leave, the people were starved for cultural information, the people are extremely curious and in awe of us, the happiness of the people and their pleasure of our visits were heartwarming. We were accorded much aplomb, too much attention and fanfare. After a gala sendoff, what we mean to them is difficult to conceive.

Out of the swarm and free at last. Although it was a test of patience and endurance, the whirling storm eventually calmed and the sun broke through. The end product of busy bees is honey, its taste rich and sweet. My thoughts and memories of those gracious and generous people leave a delectable taste that lingers.

Our group-study-exchange tour came to an end, but our Rotary hosts generously arranged for our team to visit one last site. We departed Punjab for Agra to see a structure known as one of the great wonders of the world, the Taj Mahal. If there is another structure as strikingly and as majestically beautiful as the Taj, it must be in Heaven.

Shah Jahan had it built as a memorial to his wife, Munoz. When she died in 1621 during the birth of her 14th child, Jahan was so distraught he began planning her memorial, which took 20,000 workers 20 years to build. A love story unsurpassed.

We arrived there on a Sunday afternoon, and the first view was another one of those take-your-breath-away moments. The next morning before daybreak, we walked the couple of miles from our hotel to the site. Sitting in solitude by the reflecting pool, we watched the sun come up, softly turning the pure-white marbled structure into a veil of glistening gold. My trip to India, layered in gold.

❖ ❖ ❖

Three months later, the team from District 3090 in Punjab, whose members we'd met on our visit, including my unforgettable new friend, Rao, arrived in our district. OK, first, we'll feed and feed them some more, get back at them. They nibbled on our food. Our soups, salads, fruits and vegetables were blah to them. OK, we'll add spices and marinate the rice and broccoli in a heavy dose of curry. It worked.

When I asked their team to name a special place they would like to see, the response was, "A sky-scraper, we don't have them in India." I know, and you don't have a traffic system there either. Using our traffic system, which is frequently grid locked, I took them 300 miles to Chicago. If they were fascinated riding on an interstate, what would be their reaction when they took the express elevator to the top of the Sears Tower?

It was a late April afternoon when the elevator door opened and we stepped out into an unreal world. They were mesmerized with the view, and I with their reaction and response. Looking down on the setting sun, we watched dusk begin to settle on this vast city by the lake. Soon the lights began to appear as if scattered and sown by a mystical power. The faintly twinkling lights glimmering below us were as jewels sprinkled into patterns of stars in a dark night. From the plains of India to a tower high above, my friends, initially in a trance, began to live a dream.

Early one morning three months before, our team watched the sunrise on a memorial built by a man for his wife, an unsurpassed expression of devotion and love. In the tower, we saw this same sun set in a great city, a precious gift we shared that late evening. The same source of that light would soon come up again to shine on their homeland. A few hours later, it would shine on ours. In the dusk, lights like stars from the heavens appeared from the earth below, which is the home we all share. Together, we watched the day's light dim and then saw the city come alive again. Will there ever be a time when all people see the same light? There was that brief time when one newly formed family became one.

CHAPTER 9

IT WAS MYSTICAL AND MAGICAL

❖ ❖ ❖

During retirement, after you light one fuse and it burns out, it's merely a matter of jogging to the hardware store and replenishing your fuse supply. If there's a bookstore in the vicinity, stop by and fill up your backpack.

When I read books about fascinating places, I reach for another match. After reading several books about Tibet, I had to make the journey. *Lost Horizon* by James Hilton, *Seven Years in Tibet* by Heinrich Harrer and *My Journey to Lhasa* plus *Magic and Mystery in Tibet* by Alexandra David-Neel, all utterly fascinating, resulted in another blast off. As Hilton described the fictitious *Lost Horizon,* which was undoubtedly in reference to the isolated and mysterious Tibet, I traveled there and discovered the original Shangri-La.

If you choose to read only one book about Tibet, I recommend *My Journey to Lhasa.* Alexandra David-Neel was born in France, had been an opera singer, studied Eastern languages, religions and philosophy and traveled widely in the Far East. In 1923, at age 55, (perhaps after retiring) she was the first European woman to enter Tibet's forbidden city of Lhasa. She disguised herself as a Tibetan, dyeing her hair black with ink, darkening her face and skin with charcoal and dressing in the ethnic tattered garb disguising herself as a pilgrim. She took a young Sikkimese lama (monk) with her as a companion and helper, and they traveled from the north by foot during a brutal winter. Her book is a vivid account of her incredible journey and a remarkable portrait of Tibet, its religion and people.

Not only had Lhasa been considered a forbidden city, entry to Tibet had been discouraged for centuries. It was relatively easy to keep invaders and other inquisitive people out due to the terrain. To enter Tibet from the south in Nepal, it's necessary to cross the "impossible" Himalayas. From the north, the vast plateau and sparsely populated wastelands and deserts, including the Gobi and others, are a very difficult barrier to an easily accessible entry. Very few outsiders or trespassers had walked on Tibetan soil until a scattered few sneaked in during the early 1900's. Then under Chinese jurisdiction in the mid-1900's, outsiders were strictly limited until around the 1990's.

From the south on the plains of India and the foothills in Nepal, as well as from the Tibetan plateau from the north, when going from a lower altitude to a much higher level, the first view of the Himalayas is absolutely stunning. The snow-capped jagged wall rises to unbelievable heights as if, when raising your hand, the thumb and fingers would be sticking up two feet tall. My first glimpse and impression of these inspiring, pointed spires reaching up to the heavens was—this isn't real!

As were most all my previous traveling companions, my new friends were delightful and interesting people. The group of 16 included two lawyers, a pathologist, a dentist, a stockbroker, a photographer from Vancouver, a newspaper publisher and a former Broadway actress who was a psychoanalyst. You never know when or where you might need a lawyer, stockbroker, dentist, pathologist or a psychoanalyst. The expertise I offered was how to grow tobacco, milk cows and survive 33 years of beating your brains out trying to educate America's wild and crazy youth.

Tibet is the most beautiful country in the world and perhaps my favorite of all the places I've visited. Not only is the landscape dramatic and stunningly beautiful, the Tibetan people are incredibly friendly, compassionate and peace loving. Three years after my retirement, I made the journey because I wanted to see it, particularly the Potala, the massive Buddhist palace on the side of a mountain overlooking the small, quaint city of Lhasa. With a new interest in Buddhism and the Tibetan culture, I wanted to visit that fascinating part of the world and learn how to attain Nirvana. Three years prior to my visit to Tibet, I'd been at the south face of Mt. Everest in Nepal, the account of which is in chapter four.

As mentioned in that chapter, when leaving Everest I had one of those nagging urges—how would it look from the north? Making the trip to Tibet was a way to kill four birds with one stone—tour the massive Potala Palace, visit other monasteries, see how the people live and view Everest from the north. However, you can't kill birds in Tibet. Tibetan Buddhists have compassion and reverence for all sentient (living) beings, as the Dalai Lama often reminds us. The Chinese don't. We were traveling in a land rover on a rocky, dirt road, and came upon a flock of cautious partridges ambling across our path. The driver stopped to let them pass and remarked, "The Chinese would try to run them over."

One of the greatest tragedies of the 20th Century was China's invasion of Tibet in 1951. The most compassionate and peace-loving people on earth were conquered by the Chinese Communists and remain under their subjugation. Since the Communists consider religion as "the opium of the people," the Chinese bombed and destroyed thousands of Buddhist monasteries perched upon remote mountainsides throughout the land. A few were spared, including the Potala Palace, an architectural wonder with 13 stories and over 1,000 rooms. Construction was finished in 1693, and the palace has been the primary residence of all Dali Lamas from 1755 to 1959 when the current Dalai Lama (Tenzin Gyatso) escaped in secrecy by horseback one dark night from his beloved land and has resided in India since that time.

As one indication of the extensive devastation, which was intended to wipeout their culture, the art treasures were the first to go. The Dali Lama's older brother, Takster Rimpoche explained: "First, they catalogued what was in every temple and monastery, and pillaged everything. The first wave carried away the small artworks made of precious metals or jewels. The next wave carried away things made of semi-precious materials. The third wave took away the next most precious material, such as silk brocades used to frame the paintings. The fourth wave carried away statues made of bronze or copper. Like this, they gradually and systematically stole everything from us. In the end, only bare stone walls were left. Then they came with dynamite and leveled these in order to get to the wood used as supports in the structure. In the end only rubble was left."

Tibetan Buddhism is not considered a religion as such, but more a philosophy or way of life. After being enlightened at around 500 B.C., Siddharta Gautama, the Buddha, based his teachings on Four Noble Truths: 1. Unenlightened existence is fraught with dissatisfaction and suffering, 2. Suffering is caused by desire of and attachment to material things, 3. There is a way to release and cease this suffering, and 4. The way is to detach and release those desires of fleeting and impermeable things to attain peace of mind, oneness with the universe and ultimately enlightenment. In order to enter into a state where there is no desire or suffering, one must follow an eightfold path, which includes right view, thought, speech, behavior, livelihood, effort, mindfulness, and concentration.

In other words, an entertainment center in each room, a three-car garage and a robotic carpet sweeper won't make us happy. A cell phone can actually cause suffering. The Dalai Lama explained that when you get a new car, you're happy, but the next day, you see a scratch on the hood, and then you are unhappy. Taking it to a body shop provides the opportunity to pause from the hectic life to meditate while you wait.

After boarding the plane for Tibet, I recorded in my journal:

"Another journey, the third time to the Himalayas. It's not as exciting as the others, but I want to see the Potala and Tibet. Will probably go back again to the mountains. (I did). Trekking is the thing."

After a 14-hour flight from Los Angeles on August 11, 1993, I arrived in Hong Kong on August 13. How August 12 vanished, I'll never know. After 25 sleepless hours in airports and on planes, sleep should be baby-like, but it isn't. After crashing in the hotel in a numbing stupor, I awoke three hours later at 3:00 a.m. Under such physically and psychologically deranged conditions, one's body and psyche cries out for relief. I put on my clothes, walked out into the deep, dark Hong Kong night in search of a cup of coffee. You guessed it; one block away, an all-night McDonald's was serving the same coffee they serve everywhere else except the moon. It's only a matter of time.

After our group had all rendezvoused in Hong Kong, we flew to Chengdu, China and boarded a bus for a tour to a small zoo. I'd been to all sorts of zoos, but never one that had only a single species of an animal. Observing 10 pandas observing you can take hours. What a show! Pandas can't be real—they must be something Walt Disney created.

Food is important to me. If I go without it for an extended period of time, like a short segment of a day or night, I can eat what pandas eat, bamboo. After the very long day, I was famished. They took us to a Chengdu restaurant specializing in Sichaun food. Assuming Sichaun food would be similar to Deep South food, I was in for a surprise. I admit to being raised in the sticks of Kentucky, but most of the time we used forks, spoons and knives to eat with, except fried chicken, ears of corn and watermelon. We were poor, but never had to resort to a pair of sticks to pick up a soup bean. I got nervous watching my new, refined friends corralling rice with chopsticks like it was a gob of cornbread. When no one was looking, I took the two sticks, stabbed at a piece of something and cautiously caressed it to my open mouth like I used to shoot a basketball with nothing but net. Starvation is a good teacher. Chinese food in China is about as good as the food I grew up on, like a breakfast of a thick slab of home-cured country ham, three fried eggs fresh from the henhouse, fried potatoes and biscuits covered with gravy and then more biscuits covered with churned butter and sorghum molasses to top it off.

After a night in Chengdu, I arose at 4:30 a.m. for the flight to Lhasa. I switched on the TV at that early hour and the PGA golf tournament back in the states was on. My recorded observation: "TV has changed the world." Prior to CNN, BBC and other channels going worldwide in the early 90s, the billions of the masses had no idea what the outside world was like, but they do now.

Because of strong and shifting winds at Lhasa, the airport, which is one landing strip and a hut for a terminal, is 60 miles south of the city. After landing, we departed the plane and walked very slowly to our land rovers. If you walk at four-mph at a normal pace, you'll walk one-mph at 12,000 feet. The sudden change is like stepping through an invisible wall. Enter Tibet and you're on, as it's known, "the roof of the world."

First impressions are lasting impressions. Our vehicles stopped alongside the rocky road, and we heard beautiful songs drifting across the valley. A group of Tibetan women was harvesting grain in a nearby field, singing as they worked, their melodious, sweet songs were as a welcome speech, a presentation of a golden key to their wonderful land.

It was not the last time we heard singing. Despite the cold, calculating jurisdiction of the conquering Chinese, the Tibetan people seem to maintain that vital spirit, praising life with gleeful thoughts and expressions, compassion tempered with peace and joy. Are Buddhists happier than Christians, Jews and Muslims? They certainly seem to be.

Approaching Lhasa a few miles out, we spotted the Potala hovering over the little city. My recorded first impression: "What a sight! It's bigger than the pictures reveal."

After a long day and the touchdown at 12,000-feet, we checked in at an adequate hotel. It was another one of those sudden adjustments to high altitude without time for acclimatization. The welcome to the roof of the world was like taking three hard blows to the stomach, lungs and head. My notes described the feeling: "headache and dizziness, some of the group getting sick. A tiring day and 12,000 feet leaves me blah, a tasteless dinner and to bed dead tired and aching."

If the U.S. is ever conquered by a foe determined to destroy our religion, they'll bomb most or all of our churches, synagogues and mosques. In the goodness of their heart, they might leave a few for posterity. We'll bomb the Capitol, the Pentagon and the White House, but we'll leave the National Cathedral. Sources claim the Chinese had the Potala on their list, but it was not bombed. A beacon of love and peace still shines under the life-giving sun.

Early the next morning, despite throbs shooting through our heads and dizzy butterflies fluttering in our stomachs, we climbed the seemingly unending steps up the mountain to the Potala. The notes from my journal describe my impressions:

"Ambled through the dark upper corridors, shrines, and cubbyholes crowded with eager pilgrims with butter lamps, prayer wheels and offerings. Saw the elaborately decorated stupas of the 5th and 13th Dali Lamas in the top red-painted part of the Potala. The building is so imposing, more powerful than all the pictures. One must wonder about its unknown history, the intrigue, and the spiritual dimensions reflecting from its prominent setting. Those who built it were inspired by a powerful force."

As we exited the building out into brilliant sunshine, a group of young Tibetan ladies was replacing the stones on one of the walkways. Their joyous songs echoed up through the steep walls of this ancient, massive edifice.

Rising at 4:30 the next morning, we traveled five miles to the Drepung monastery. Before the Chinese takeover, more than 8,000 monks from all over Tibet were housed there to study Buddhist philosophy and literature. Now, there are about 400 monks residing at Drepung on the one day of each year when a large thanka is unfurled on the mountainside above the monastery. Many of these tapestries of various sizes hang in most all monasteries, shrines and temples. We were fortunate to be there on the one special day each year. Upon daybreak, thousands of Tibetan pilgrims, coming from afar, assembled on the mountainside and gathered around the site where the thanka was to be unveiled. A thanka is a tapestry depicting the Buddha and various other deities. Mounds of incense burned around the site in the early-morning mist, raising sheets of smoky veils up toward the heavens. A long procession of monks, with musical instruments and colorful banners, began their slow march up the valley. Sounds of praise from horns, conch shells, drums and cymbals rang out through the valley.

After arriving at the site, we were invited and guided by a monk to the rooftop of the monastery. From there, the view of the ceremony was magnificent. Excitement filled the air as the drama unfolded. As the approximately 50 by 100 foot thanka was slowly unfurled, revealing brilliant colors of red, gold, white, blue, brown and green, it slid slowly and deliberately down over the mountain side. Four smaller deities were depicted in each corner of the thanka with the massive Buddha in the center sitting in his familiar meditative pose. Imagine a sunrise on Easter morning, observing thousands of worshippers as clergy unveil a massive work of art depicting the Resurrection.

After less than an hour, the thanka was rolled up for another year. Many of the devout Buddhists and thousands of pilgrims lingered and then walked the Kora, which is a sacred path around the monastery. A young monk invited three of us to his small and relatively clean living quarters. He was gracious, excited and pleased to host us, and, of course, we somewhat reluctantly accepted and drank a couple of hot cups of yak-butter tea. What an opportunity and what a day!

We hung around Lhasa the next day, visited a couple of other nearby monasteries and visited the Jokhang in the center of Lhasa, which is the most sacred temple in Tibet. Tibetans make pilgrimages there perhaps somewhat like Muslims make to Mecca.

Our hosts treated us to an original Tibetan dinner the night before leaving Lhasa. We were served chang, a mild milky beer made from barley, butter tea, Tibetan cheese, tsampa (barley), yak tongue, yak stomach and many other dishes flavored with very strong yak butter. If I were isolated on an island and had to choose between yak tongue or yak stomach to survive, it would be a very difficult decision. How long can one last fasting?

Early the next morning, we loaded up in four land cruisers, tossed our supplies in a truck, which also carried our Sherpas, and drove on an incredible 15-day journey through Tibet. We camped in tents and ate tasty meals prepared by our cook, Pemba.

My description of one camp: "We drove four hours up a rough valley road. The campsite was in an extraordinary setting with a roaring river in front, nomadic herders camping across the river in their dark, black tents made of yak hair, and the Drigung monastery perched halfway up on a mountain about a mile up the valley."

In reviewing my journal, practically every daily entry included these descriptive terms: magnificent setting, incredible site, fantastic, dramatic view and the happy people.

There are no roads as such in the Tibetan countryside, only rocky, dusty, muddy, snow covered or icy trails. Our rugged land rovers went places where walking would be difficult, through streams, up steep slopes and around precipitous cliffs. We stopped at a few small villages and every couple of days visited another monastery, those few which hadn't been destroyed or were being reconstructed.

At one campsite, four of our group walked a trail about three miles up on a mountainside to visit a small nunnery perched on a scenic ledge. A nunnery is a monastery for female lamas, or anis as they are known. Despite its remote site, the Chinese also destroyed this nunnery, which housed over 100 anis at that time. It was like target practice—fun and exciting. Zoom your fighter plane down through the tall mountains and drop a couple bombs. Nothing to worry about; they can't shoot back. Bingo!

The nunnery was partially reconstructed, and 12 anis came out to greet us. One was older than the others, who all appeared to be under the age of 30. Dressed in the familiar maroon and gold robes, with their coal-black hair cut in "burr" `style, it was a bit difficult to determine if they were male or female. When I noticed the windows in their nunnery were perfectly clean, and they continued giggling, I knew they were female. With our guide and lead Sherpa, Ang Porba serving as interpreter, we made small talk and, of course, were compelled to drink a cup of the familiar yak-butter tea.

The nunnery stood in front of a cave entrance for a purpose. Lamas spend three weeks, three months and up to three years meditating in caves. We were informed that one ani was missing the party; it was her turn to meditate. Such is the magic and mystery of Tibet.

After a most gracious welcome and visit, and after gawks, giggles and the butter tea, it was time to bid farewell. I reached into my pocket full of hard candies wrapped in cellophane and began handing one to each ani. They seemed hesitant and puzzled, but Ang Porba explained what they had received. As we departed down the mountain, the anis had huddled together, boisterously chatting, giggling and comparing each little piece of candy. Such small gifts are often remembered for the longest time. I vividly remember their expressions of gratitude and their pleasure and happiness at our surprising visit.

After walking back to camp, having dinner, and a peaceful sleep, we awakened to another day of magic and mystery. After a couple hours on the rough, dirt road, we stopped again and looked up. About 50 huge vultures were staring down at us from a meadow up on the side of a mountain. We climbed up to a small stupa where a caretaker lama dwelled. His responsibility was to complete the process for a "sky burial." Upon death, it's a great honor for a worthy Buddhist to be buried in this fashion. Only a select few are rewarded. The vultures remained on the slope only a 100 feet or so above us. Calm and patient, there was no need for them to fly away. A few wild dogs hovered a couple hundred feet above them. They were not waiting to attack the vultures; but waiting for something else.

Upon death, an honorable and worthy one's body is carried to the burial spot, which is approximately a 10 by 10 foot square layer of stones placed on the ground. The caretaker then chops the body, both flesh and bones, into small pieces and sprinkles it with ground tsampa. By way of Ang Porba's interpretation, the caretaker assured us the wild dogs were not permitted to participate. But why were they waiting there? Perhaps in deepest, darkest night they would move in and clean up any remaining morsels after the vultures completed the sky-burial ceremony. The birds devour the flesh, fly away to the heavens and deposit the soul's physical remains back into the good earth. Thus, the life cycle endures.

When our caravan stopped in the middle of nowhere, it was obvious we'd encountered something mysterious. However, it was not a mystery that our supply truck was stuck in the rapids of a mountain stream. We had two choices, call AAA or build a bridge. The nearest AAA was in San Francisco, so we built a bridge. Forming a human chain up the side of the mountain, we passed hundreds of rocks down and threw them under the truck. It takes about three hours to build a makeshift bridge across a small stream in the Himalayas. It takes 30 years to see all of Tibet.

What's that up ahead? It appears to be people falling down and getting up, then falling down and getting up. Strange, but that's what they were doing. A very attractive family of two brothers and three sisters, appearing to be between 20 and 30 years of age, were making a pilgrimage to Lhasa. They had been on the pilgrimage for six months with one month to go. Their journey was a long, slow process, because their devotion to the Buddha way required them to prostrate themselves throughout their long, arduous route.

Each wore a long leather apron covering the fronts of their bodies. The young pilgrims also wore protective shields on the palms of each hand, made from pieces of thick wood. We learned each of them had already worn out five pairs of these wooden coverings. They were pleased to see us, and after a bit of rest, interpreted conversation and photos, they resumed their quest.

In a single line, the pilgrims would take a couple of steps, fall forward with the wooden shields attached to their hands striking the ground first and then slide down to the earth on the fronts of their bodies. After a brief pause, up again, down again, up and down repeatedly for six months and only one more month to go. I recorded: "Devotion without limits."

If 150 million Americans, who need to lose weight, would prostrate themselves an hour each day, the sweet shops would close and the fast food joints would go out of business.

Having accomplished three of my goals—touring Lhasa and the Potala, seeing how the Tibetan people live and visiting several monasteries—only one goal remained. I was on my way to see Mt. Everest from the north. We rounded a bend and there it was, the Mother Goddess of the Earth, an apt description of the all-imposing, reigning peak. Was the view more spectacular from the south or the north? Was your first baby more beautiful from the left or the right side?

To get to Everest from the south, it takes over a week to walk from the airstrip at Lukla. From the north, it's a drive, five mph at times, over treacherous road, but directly to the base camp. About a mile before arriving at camp, we passed by the Rongbuk monastery, the highest monastery in the world at 16,500 feet. If you're thinking of becoming a Buddhist monk, you might want to consider Rongbuk, especially if you'd like to spend your life studying, chanting and meditating in a walk-in deep freeze. We set up camp in a 50-tent city on the Rongbuk glacier. Two other expeditions, which were preparing to climb the highest mountain hovering above us, were also camped there.

The day after our arrival, I recorded: "It's been a grand day in my life." I've had many grand days. Although I don't remember it, my birthday has to rank at the top. All my workdays were grand ones, too, especially when the boss said, "It's quittin' time." There is no quitting time during the retirement days, and who wants to quit retirement? You'd have to rewrite your resume' or fade into that eternal retirement where they cancel your Social Security resulting in the end of a social life on earth. Retirement is, or should be, one very good day after another. I've discovered that if you are ardently pursuing an active and adventurous retirement, the grand days begin to pile up.

Ang Porba led me to this grand day. He was our sirdar, the head Sherpa of our group and a remarkable man. At age 21 in 1979, he was the youngest person to climb Mt. Everest. During that climb, two other climbers froze to death. He explained that after his team had successfully descended, another team struggled. He could see them trying to make it down. Their Sherpa tried desperately to help them, but to no avail. The Sherpa finally made it back to camp despite severe snow blindness and frozen toes. These extraordinarily strong people perform amazing feats. The Sherpa continues leading climbers up the mountain, without toes. Ang Porba made five other attempts, and although he climbed to within a few hundred feet from the top, he never reached the summit again. (An account of this grand day when Ang Porba took me to a summit is presented in the last chapter.)

After breakfast, we packed up and departed for the two-day journey back to Kathmandu, and the end of our amazing adventure. Traveling down from the high mountains to the foothills was a continuation of fabulous scenery. In the moist, misty and lush setting, two or three long, narrow waterfalls from each high mountain cascaded down to the valleys from the higher altitudes. Each bend in the road was another magical scene.

We arrived at the border of Tibet and Nepal and, after being thoroughly checked by Chinese border guards, walked across the Friendship Bridge to the small village of Zangmu. The plumbing at the Zangmu Hotel, where I awoke during the night with a leach attached to my leg, had not worked since probably soon after the hotel was constructed. Oh, well. We'd used trees, rocks and ravines for three weeks, so what's the big deal when you have to go? The rooms did have windows.

The next morning we piled all our gear and our "dirty" bodies into an old rattle-trap bus. The driver, who appeared to be too young for a driver's license, had been anxiously gunning the motor. He had a young lady of perhaps 16 standing beside him near the driver's seat. The reason—she was the person operating the brake. Whenever the young driver needed to slow down going around a death-defying curve with a 3,000-foot drop off, she would grab the emergency brake and pull up with all her might. Did the bus have the kind of brakes you push down with a foot? Apparently, not. The brakes had probably burned out years ago, and parts are scarce out in the middle of nowhere.

When you retire and travel to exotic places, be prepared for chills, thrills and potential spills. When traveling over mountainous roads in vehicles best suited for a junkyard, realize your life is solely in the hands of the Almighty. Close your eyes and pray there will be another light of day.

What's that up ahead? It appears to be mud about as high as the 13th floor of the Empire State Building. It was. A recent landslide had covered the road with another of nature's wonders, a humongous mudslide, which tends to follow the law of gravity. What do we do now? We can either sit in the bus for months or pack up all our gear and climb up over the massive slide. Our faithful Sherpas and porters loaded most of our gear on their backs, carrying the heaviest loads. Our group had no other choice but to climb. It was difficult for those who were in poorer shape, but after a difficult three-hour climb over boulders and up steep inclines, we made it to the other side and waiting buses.

It was near dark when we arrived in Kathmandu and the Shangri La Hotel. Hot showers, clean clothes and a wonderful dinner topped off the long, long day, and a journey like no other.

I'll miss my tent, a temporary home, but one nonetheless. I'll miss Pemba's food, which was something like Hemingway's "movable feast." A hotel window lets in a little light, but is restraining and limiting. When you awaken to a new day, unzip the tent and look out on a wondrous world with the sun rising over the highest peaks amidst the revitalizing brisk morning air, you view spaces unlimited with horizons endless.

I'll miss my new friends, my Sherpas and Ang Porba. I'll miss the joyous songs echoing from the villages and grain fields. I'll miss the monks and the monasteries, the chanting and the prayer wheels. I'll miss the beautiful way of life as Tibetans live it, the core of which exemplifies grace, peace and compassion.

Goodbye, and on to Hong Kong and the 15-hour flight to Los Angeles. One day, you're free and unrestrained; the next day, "Fasten your seat belt." A 747 seat is unlike a sleeping bag in a tent. "Do you want a pillow?" No, I rest better with my head on the earth. The Buddha did not use an airplane to soar through the friendly skies.

CHAPTER 10

A BLANK ON A MAP

❧ ❧ ❧

Veteran retirees tend to avoid what's next, if it's exerting, surprising or shocking. We have only three basic rules to follow: 1. Get up, 2. Survive, and 3. Go to bed. Sounds simple, but it isn't. The survival rule is the toughest one to follow. A typical day: Go see the doctor, who recommends a specialist, who recommends tests. While waiting, read health tips in year-old magazines. While you're out, pick up pre-scriptions, stop by a mall, grab a senior-discounted happy meal, buy skim milk and bran and then, being overcome with drowsiness, rush home to nap in preparation for happy hour. A half-and-half prune juice and vodka with a celery stalk kicks more than you might think, but you get a daily serving of a fruit and vegetable. After changing channels for an hour or two, it's 9:00 p.m. and time for bed. Studies show that it takes older folks an average of 59 minutes to prepare for the sack.

Drink warm milk with your medicine, but don't confuse the one-a-day pills with those you take two, four and six times per day. It's also helpful to remember pill colors—red is blood pressure, pink is inflammation and blue is anxiety. Undress, grab a hot compound and rub it vigorously and deeply into your pulled muscles. After washing the hot-rub from your hands, put your partial teeth in a glass of salt water and relieve your bladder by squeezing it. Then get dressed in something like an Eskimo suit for warmth and go to bed by jumping or falling in. Most old people can't jump so they fall. You're exhausted, I know, but we're not there yet. Place your hearing aids and glasses on the table by your head and turn out the light, being cautious not to knock it over. Fumbling for the light, you knock your trifocals to the floor. Get down on your knees and crawl. When you think you've found them, it's your nasal spray. Without your knee brace in place, pull up to the bed and stand, if you can. Once you're balanced, go to the bathroom and reach for the, uh, what is it I came here to reach for? The survival rule is important to us, as is sleeping and waking up, followed by ejecting from the bed without a need for a pulley system. Close your eyes and drift into dreams about tomorrow. One last cautionary point, try not to dream about those nights 60 years ago when sex served as your sleeping pill. It will keep you wide awake.

OK, perhaps I was exaggerating. I don't drink prune juice. And there's nothing amusing about getting old and experiencing our sensory and bodily functions in decline. But what are we going to do about the reality of aging—mourn, grieve and complain to anyone who will listen? I could explain my ailments in two chapters, but this book is not about fall and decline, it's about rising up.

Although going to bed and waking up can be a hassle, it's what we do in between that matters. The survival segment of each day should be a kind of survival-of-the-fittest quest, using and strengthening every individual part of us that is fit. What's surprising is that Darwin was right; if the will is fit, the chance of survival improves. Or was that God's theory?

Despite my energy tank being half-full, apprehension about my knees and 68 years of body wear, I trekked to the advanced base camp at K2, the second tallest mountain in the world. It was as easy as climbing an 18,000-foot frozen pie topped with thick chunks of white ice and whipped-cream snow. Preparing for bed took less than a minute. I simply fell into a sleeping bag enclosed in a tent frequently being whipped and blown by a windstorm. A dirt mattress is more comfortable than one composed of rocks. The advantage of a glacial mattress is that it prevents night sweats.

K2 is located in the extreme western part of China near the Pakistan, Tajikistan and Afghanistan borders. Most climbers and trekkers approach K2 from the south through Pakistan, which is the easier and more accessible route. However, in 2002, with the turbulent and uncertain conditions in Pakistan, climbing and trekking expeditions had been limited to the northern route.

Our sponsor, Wilderness Travel, arranged for our group to attack from the north, a longer and more arduous route. They explained: "We have completed significant scouting for this new adventure, but unlike the majority of our trips, K2 and the Chinese Karakorum is a first-time exploratory and thus requires a flexible attitude and willingness to occasionally 'expect the unexpected.' It is a long trek in a very remote region and is designed for those who are adventurous in body and spirit."

I have a flexible attitude up to a point and live my life expecting the unexpected. My body and spirit are conditioned to go off a deep end on occasion, so count me in.

If you decide to go to K2, get a map and pack two bags. The clothing and equipment list includes 39 essential items. Optional items include cameras, batteries, trekking poles, books, small tools, binoculars, snacks and a sewing kit. It requires considerable arm-strength to stuff all this gear into two bags.

The quickest way to get there is to fly to Beijing, China, then to Urumgi and from there to Kashgar. You're not there yet, and, after landing, you must ride a land rover for two days through part of the Taklimakan Desert to where the dirt road, sprinkled with grapefruit-size rocks, ends. The fun actually begins at that point when you walk for 10 days—up, over, down and up, up—to the Advanced Base Camp. There's K2, so turn around and go back home the same way you came.

Beijing is a progressive city and China was preparing for the 2008 Olympics. As soon as I walked out of the airport terminal, my eyes began burning. The haze was thick as Wonton soup. About one-third of the Chinese on the streets were wearing masks. How would an athlete ever participate in such conditions? However, when I returned to Beijing three weeks later, the air was much better and didn't scratch my nasal passages or cause my eyes to burn.

The Swisshotel in Beijing was first class and the food outstanding if you can put food in your mouth with two sticks. I'm a slow learner, but adapt quickly when food's on the table. When I was checking in, I recognized the guy in the lobby.

"Hi, Gary. Remember me?"

"I'm trying to place you."

"The Vajra Hotel in Kathmandu, 11 years ago."

"Terry, you mailed my Christmas cards."

Gary McCue lives in Tasmania and has led high and adventurous treks throughout the Himalayas and the Karakorum for over 20 years. He speaks Hindi and is conversant in Tibetan and Chinese. He is a great guy, as were my other six traveling companions, except Barbara wasn't a guy. She was a lady from Boston and tough as any guy on the trek. John was a consultant from Illinois, Robert, a businessman from Florida, Art worked for Boeing in Seattle and Randy lived near Washington and work in national security. When I asked what he did, he replied, "I can't tell you, except every morning I read communiqués, and they scare the hell out of me." David ran a language software company in Cambridge, Mass. He had Ph.D.'s seeping from his skull; more about him later.

After the group had all arrived, we had our first meeting. Gary asked, "Is everyone ready for another exciting adventure?" It was certainly that, and I wouldn't have traded the experience for a winning lottery ticket. Life is an adventure, or nothing.

We spent a couple days in Beijing touring the incredible Forbidden City, Tinnamon Square and Mao's tomb, and they took us to see a wall. What were they thinking? There's no way to keep invaders out, as we've discovered with our leaky Great Fence running over parts of the Mexican border. The Great Wall is truly a wonder of wonders.

China, a vast land with over a billion people, is on the move and moving fast. Construction is ongoing everywhere. Tear down the old and build a new. Tear down every centuries-old, uniquely distinct culture and do it our way. Four years after my stopover in Urumgi, protests and violence broke out between the native Uguirs and the Han Chinese. Not only is the conflict cultural, it's primarily economic. Chinese get the jobs and drive cars while the natives scratch out a meager living on the land and ride on donkey carts.

To attract tourists and businesses, build hotels and restaurants. On our stopover in Urumgi, my nice modern hotel room had a TV in the bedroom and a TV in an adjoining smaller sitting room. The breakfast buffet provided Chinese breakfast foods on one table and what you'd get at a New York Hilton on the other. Although native Chinese food is wonderfully delicious, their breakfast foods are not. In Urumgi, Kashgar and on the road to begin our trek, the food was excellent. We had meals of meat-filled dumplings, noodles and rice with tasty sauces and kabobs of spiced mutton that were delicious. In Kashgar, I ate many slices of melon that were superior to any I'd ever eaten. It was the size of a small oblong watermelon with bright yellow flesh succulent as nectar from the gods.

After a day and night in Urumgi, we flew to Kashgar, an ancient Silk Road small city in the extreme western part of China. Historically, Kashgar is noted for its markets. People from surrounding areas crowd several streets lined with an array of stalls filled with goods for sale. On the outskirts during Saturdays, a livestock market including sheep, goats, cattle, donkeys and poultry is as busy. New construction surrounds the ancient parts of the city, and wide new streets have replaced dusty lanes. Despite modernization, about half of the travel on the new streets, some of which are four lanes, are two-wheeled carts pulled by a donkey and loaded with family members and produce. It was a page from the horse and buggy days when Henry Ford first entered the scene.

I've been to many cities, but had never seen the latest in traffic lights. In Kashgar, where camel trains once caused gridlock on the Silk Road, the stoplights have a digital clock attached. When it turns green, the clock ticks off the seconds before the light turns red. Could I make it across in eight seconds, before colliding with a donkey?

It was a two-day trip in land rovers to the end of the road. The first night we stopped in the small town of Ye Cheng and checked in at the Ye Cheng

Electricity Hotel, (that's what the sign said). After going to our rooms, the electricity went off.

Soon after the land rovers dumped us out at the endpoint of the bouncy road, or whatever it was, I saw a man and a boy walking toward our camp with twelve Bactrian camels following in single file. "Camel Man," as we called him, was from nearby Tajikistan. He was as tough as a camel, with the courage and confidence of a lion. He and his young helper slept out under the stars during the coldest nights snuggled under pads with their camels lying nearby.

One advantage of using camels as pack animals, compared to yaks, donkeys or llamas, is camels will let you ride them snuggly between their two humps. They are very strong animals and can carry up to 800 pounds. We waded through several ice-cold streams, but we hopped aboard the camels to cross the ones waist deep. When Camel Man gave the commands, the camel would kneel down, we'd climb aboard and it was smooth sailing. No, it was rough sailing.

At that time, one year after 9/11, word was that bin Laden and his Al-Qaeda cohorts were hiding out in the area. There couldn't be a better place to hide, but I didn't see him or signs of human life other than our group and a few Chinese soldiers in a small military outpost. Near the end of our first day's trek, we rounded a bend and saw a small compound behind a high fence. A small number of the Chinese army was on the lookout for terrorists or invaders. Do we look like mad bombers, or I, with a white beard, resemble bin Laden? After a thorough check of our documents near a fenced kennel enclosing two man-eating Shepherd dogs near the size of camels, they let us pass.

With no other human beings in sight, our journey took us under magnificent snow-capped mountains, down through deep valleys and endless desolation. It was miles and miles of a no-man's land. Not only is the vast area practically uninhabitable, it's inhospitable. Wander off and be devoured.

Three Cups of Tea, the fascinating, best-selling book published in 2006, tells the incredible story of Greg Mortenson. Early in the account, Mortenson, disoriented and weakened, became lost on two occasions when returning to a small village after an unsuccessful attempt to climb K2. The landscape is such that to veer off a trail means being swallowed in an endless maze. Mortenson's team approached K2 from the south in Pakistan: our group from the north, which is even more desolate. A Balti clan of people, who lived in a small, remote village in Pakistan, rescued Mortenson and nursed him back to health. The village chief told him, "Here (in Pakistan and Afghanistan) we drink three cups of tea to do business; the first, you are a stranger, the second, you become a friend, and the third, you join our family, and for our family we are prepared to do anything—even die."

After the second cup of tea with most all the native people I've become friends with during my travels, I felt acceptance beyond expectation. Love thy neighbor seems to be universal when based on a foundation of humanity's natural bonds. Prejudice and greed foster aggression and prohibit building a family of man. I've walked many miles alongside those of diverse cultures and varied faiths—Buddhists, Muslims, Hindus, Christians and non-believers as well. A journey together toward a common destination revealed to me—two hearts beat as one.

Although arid and bleak, the landscape was captivating and mesmerizing. Hiking or climbing over precarious, steep, and difficult terrain required following the life-preservation rule—if you look up, you may go down. We hiked over several passes in the 16,000-foot range, and then down to wide riverbeds, up and down. On the riverbeds, some at least a half-mile wide, I never looked up. The numbers of rocks and pebbles slammed, formed and smoothed during centuries of nature's course were innumerable, as are the grains of sand on a beach. They are designed in varied shapes, sizes and colors. With each focused step I took on nature's pristine rocky road, I wanted to put this one in my pack—no that one. A pack is not a dump truck. As I walked over miles of riverbeds, there was no escape from a recurring thought; this part of the world was reserved for me to get a brief glimpse of a part of nature's grand plan.

Everyday, I see two small rocks on my desk staring back at me. One is a small sand-colored rock with a distinct black question mark naturally embedded in the center. It reminds me of the eternal question, "Why?" The other one is coal black with a near perfect, pure-white cross in the center. The only explanation I have for going there was to find those two rocks, and to replenish that unfilled part of me which satisfies and sustains my eager and wandering spirit.

Back to reality and a practical concern. Where and what would our camels eat? Camel Man knows. The whole area was practically devoid of vegetation, except in scattered places near the rivers. We camped primarily in those areas for two reasons; it's where life-sustaining water flowed and dinner for the camels grew, scrubby, prickly bushes for our camels to devour—leaves stems and all.

The 14th day into the trek was 9/11, one year after "the" 9/11. I recorded:

"Some thoughts of 9/11, but it is amazing how one becomes oblivious to the outside world. The absolute lack of other people amidst near-perfect nature takes the mind from all cares other than the long, hard treks in these magnificent mountains."

After six days, we arrived at the lower base camp, a place called Suget Jangel, below the terminus of the K2 Glacier. With the exception of a few groves of stunted willow trees, the place was bare. The noted explorer Francis Youngblood was the first outsider to explore that area at the turn of the 20th century. Eric Shipton named the spot Suget Jangle and used it as his base to explore the area in 1930, as described in his classic book, *Blank on a Map*. It is. I've never spent a night in Seattle or Jersey City, but I spent five nights of my life in Suget Jangel, before and after our trek to the advanced base camp.

So far, so good. My knees held together and my lungs didn't collapse. I held my own with the younger generation until, of all things, a tooth began aching like a camel had kicked me in the mouth. I hadn't had a toothache since the Tooth Fairy days. Fortunately, the day before leaving for the advanced base camp was a rest and preparation day, or I couldn't have continued. Gary, who had extensive training in treating all kinds of ailments, gave me a powerful antibiotic from the treasured medical black bag. I felt much better, except I had been gargling hot salt water and blistered my mouth and gums. Chewing on the left side of my mouth was Chinese water torture. When I returned home, I met with a mouth specialist. He explained that high altitudes often cause problems with teeth. I knew altitude caused problems with every other part of your body, but your teeth?

Goodbye camels and downtown Suget Jangel, see you later. From 12,000 feet, we packed up the barest essentials—food, tents, sleeping bags and clothing—and started up a steep mountain on a six-day, five-night journey to and from the advanced base camp at nearly 17,000 feet. The pack on my back weighed about 45 pounds at the bottom of the mountain and what seemed like double the weight at the top, and that's without adding my rock collection.

K2 is about 1,000 miles west of Mt. Everest and 500 miles further north. Although Mt. Everest is nearly 800 feet higher, K2 is far more difficult to climb and more susceptible to violent storms, which over the years have blown many climbers to their deaths. In 2008, 11 climbers died on one expedition. In 2009, 450 climbers reached the summit of Mt. Everest. Only 296 people have ever climbed K2, with at least 77 casualties.

When asked why he did it, a climber replied, "Because it's beautiful." Sometimes I asked myself, "Why am I here?" In the mornings, I wake up and understand. Why am I here? Because it's beautiful, that's why. Whatever the ultimate purpose, God must have scattered his remarkable handiwork in proud, private places for man to see. Awakening each morning amidst a spectacular landscape, one's life turns a new page, opened to the challenge of uncovering a new gift.

After the first hard day carrying our packs toward the higher camp, up and over steep slopes, through ravines and over huge boulders, we set up camp early on a high plateau. Gary and Jiang, one of our porters, needed time to look for the best route to the base. David was my tent mate during the five nights on this part of our journey, and the most highly educated person I've ever known.

When a refreshing breeze is blowing down toward the zero degree, you can stand outside and enjoy the scenery, or go inside a 6x7-foot tent. I've been asked, "Why didn't you sit by a campfire and tell stories?" First, there are no trees above a tree line, and second, if there were, they were never used for fuel. In those conditions, it's 12 to 16 hours in a tent, and eight or 10 outside on the go. After a hard day in the elements, sleep comes naturally, up to 12 hours per night. With three or four extra hours in a tent, what does one do? If not unbearably cold, reading with a headlamp or a small light tucked in a sleeping bag is one possibility, or you could stare at canvas. The only other activity available is talking with your tent mate.

If I had to choose a (same-sex) tent mate, David would rank at the top. His hobby was writing dictionaries and encyclopedias. Not really, but he qualified with advanced degrees in linguistics from Harvard, physics from M.I.T. and philosophy from the Sorbonne in Paris. Although his early background was in music, he owned a software company, which converted other languages to English. He was married to, as he described, "the most beautiful lady in the world," a renowned choreographer from China. Now he was stuck with the oldest and ugliest guy in a tent on a moonscape glacier. David taught astronomy, physics and other sciences and was a tough trekker. He had it all. I felt like a blank spot on a map of morons.

We talked. One night I asked a question about Chinese history. I got an hour lecture on everything from the Ming Dynasty to Mao Tae-sung's long march. What could I say? Explain how to raise sheep, milk cows and cut tobacco? I could tell him how to investigate and confiscate a stash of marijuana in a student's locker, or how to turn kids on to diagramming sentences and memorizing the Gettysburg Address. Believe it our not, he wanted to know about the world I knew.

I spent good money and weeks torturing my body to see K2 and it wasn't there. When we crossed the high passes, Gary would point, indicating K2 should be right over there. God knows too much sunlight will blind a man and cause skin cancer, which necessitates periodic cloud cover, but please, God, it's enough already. Guess we'll eventually bump into it. Oh, well, I'd seen it before. Several years prior, I'd flown from Srinigar in Kashmir to New Delhi. At about 24,000 feet, the pilot directed our attention to K2. The top of its pyramid was peeking through the clouds. What a sight! Look at it this way; if I didn't get to see it from the ground this time, at least I got some exercise.

After climbing over the North Glacier and through a narrow ravine, we arrived at the Advanced Base Camp, about a quarter-mile from the base of the mountain. K2 was asleep under a thick cloud cover, apparently not wanting to be disturbed. We set up camp in an enchanting setting nestled down in a snow-white fairyland. Tall, pure-white seracs up to 40-feet high surrounded us, ridges of sharp, bright, cone-shaped pinnacles of ice pushed up over the edges of crevasses on the glacier, a winter wonderland if ever there was one.

When you are up high, remember the fluid intake rule; drink like a camel, except take the oasis with you. When up high in a tent without plumbing, what do you do after filling a liter bottle with yellow liquid from your bladder? Drink more; drink bowls of hot broth, cups of tea and water—water until you bladder is seven months pregnant. At about 3:00 a.m., I unzipped the tent flap to pour out the full bottle.

Behold! The heavens had opened. You could nearly touch K2 as it glowed in the night with two bright stars glistening on either side like candle tips sent down from a heavenly source to light the way. What a sight! The next day, we hiked in knee-deep snow the half-mile or so to its base. That night, we watched the moon come up, a bright orange beacon brushing at the tip. I can go home now, but a part of me will always remain there in the stillness, by the glowing light.

The next morning, we began the long 10-day journey back to Kashgar, and a hot shower. On a mountain where germs refuse to breed and body odors freeze, you don't need a shower. Going down is usually easier, but not on our third day. Camel Man scouted the shortest route. It was down a long and deep ravine strewn with boulders larger than trucks. Crawl up and over with the pack, and then slide down. At the end of that day, Gary, who had trekked in all parts of the mountains for over 20 years, said it was the toughest day he had ever experienced.

Civilization—showers, burgers and a house—is OK, but it gets lonely in a traffic jam. You're trapped, but not in the mountains. Trekking for 20 days, isolated and frequently alone, provides the time and conditions to reconnect with that vital part of the soul, often placed aside and neglected. Although you never stray too far from a partner or the designated route, there are stretches of time and opportunities for solitude and reflection. It's like a slow-moving meditation, an enlightened awareness of a protective power solemnly bestowing strength—and unconditional gratitude for the gift of all life, in all places. If you want to see or climb a mountain, it's stupid traveling all the way to the Eastern Hemisphere to take a hike. South America, here I come.

Gary, who had done extensive research on prior expeditions to that area, informed us we were the only trekking group to make it to the advanced base camp from the north. He also told me I was the oldest person ever there, which helped me regress in age 10 to 15 years. Consequently, I had survived so well that three years later I headed up Aconcaqua in Argentina, the highest mountain in the Western Hemisphere.

CHAPTER 11

HOW TO PREVENT RETIREMENT FAILURE

❧ ❧ ❧

Do not fail your retirement as I almost did. You can't fail if you keep working at it, and especially if there are many more things you must complete. I must write another chapter about my life, and then the next one and the one after that. I hope I'm not close to the epilogue, after which the book is closed. Failing retirement is sitting around thinking about the next chapter. Pages of blank paper are a waste of time and resources. Each successive chapter of our lives should be approached with wide-eyed anticipation. It's what makes your world spin. When the time comes to close out the book, the back cover should read, "He's resting in peace with his boots on."

According to the former humorous and homespun philosopher George Carlin, "You become 21, turn 30, push 40, reach 50 and make it to 60. You've built up so much speed that you hit 70." When hitting anything at that age, it can be a glancing blow, a sudden stop or a plunge over the edge into an abyss.

When I hit 71 with noticeably diminished speed, I attempted climbing Aconcagua in Argentina, the highest mountain in the Western Hemisphere.

Notice the word "attempted" prior to the word "climbing." I failed to make it to the top, but, thank God, didn't fail making it to the bottom, practically on my hands and knees.

Have you ever failed in school or a marriage or two? Yes, marriage is often like climbing to a peak in any hemisphere. Marriages end when husband and wife separate and divorce. When your body separates from your mind, you get divorced from climbing. The mind says, "Move your legs." The body, like an unwilling spouse, screams, "No!"

I'd made it to the advanced base camp at K2 three years prior to attempting to reach the top of Aconcagua, and had climbed to 20,000 feet four years prior to that in Bolivia. Experience enhances age, does it not? Why let aging interfere with living a full and robust life? If experience is the best teacher, you must stay enrolled in school. Aging is also a masterful teacher, if you're not too dense to learn the lessons.

"Ah, a man's reach should exceed his grasp/Or what's a heaven for?" Robert Browning understood that God's creation is a little bit of heaven at our call. To grasp the rewards, where the treasures dwell, is to reach beyond the ordinary. Once again, the awesome power of the mountains attracted and invited me, a continuing test of my will and spirit. If the spirit is willing, that's all you need. Then you begin stretching and reaching for one little twinkling star barely out of reach. Don't deny your spirit when it says, "That's OK. Try that one over there."

On January 3, 2006, on the flight to Atlanta to Santiago to Mendoza, Argentina, I recorded:

"To climb Aconcagua at 22,851. Preparation and getting the gear together was laborious. Training by running and carrying 50-pound packs up hills. Hope I'm ready. Can I do it? You never know is part of my philosophy. Why try? A challenge keeps me going."

You never know unless you give it a try, which has worked very well for me. However, at what point does one's reach become unrealistic? Place yourself on a dusty shelf and it will soon become unrealistic to climb down. As the years pass by, living is a challenge with security and longevity the goal. What is security, and why strive for longevity without purposeful and rewarding activity?

Adventuras Patagonis, a company specializing in mountain adventures, sent me a book of instructions and information including a list of 25 items of clothing for my head, hands, lower and upper body and both feet. Being summer there, it was hot at the trailhead in the valley, but "the wind chill can dip to minus 70 degrees on the summit." The sleeping bag should be rated to minus 20 degrees to prevent rigor mortis.

Following instructions, I prepared my body for the demanding physical challenge. Running to keep the cardiovascular and respiratory systems in shape was like eating a piece of fluffy cake. Two days before my departure, I ran the 10-Mile Hangover Classic on New Year's Day. Running 10 miles is harder than climbing 1,000 feet, right? Wrong. And carrying 50 pounds up the steepest nearby slopes was like carrying a 50-pound sack of potatoes from my car to the kitchen. The only difference was, my car was parked on 4,000 feet of elevation. At 20,000 feet, a sack of potatoes is a car.

Our group of 11, plus 3 guides, assembled at the first-class Hilton Hotel in Mendoza. The group included eleven men and three women with two from England, two from South Korea, two native Argentineans, seven Yankees and one Rebel. When I met my new family, I rebelled. They were all more than 25 years younger than me.

Wes, an adventurer and climbing instructor from Jackson Hole, Wyoming, was our leader assisted by Amelio from Argentina and Laura, a young lady from Oregon trained in climbing and survival. Laura's training was very important to me later in the expedition.

The welcome dinner consisted of a thick Argentinean, mouth-watering steak like kings eat, plus about 15 delicious side dishes and gallons of wine at a cost $10 without a senior discount. I avoid red meat, but not in Argentina. Apparently, their beef is raised on milk and honey.

We loaded up the gear, nearly enough to fill a freight car, and drove from the valley at Mendoza up into the mountains to Penitentes, a small village located on a road from Mendoza to Santiago. The small hotel in the village was adequate, and served thick delicious steaks, too. On the trail, noodle porridge and rice mush was the substitute for red meat.

After a night and day sorting, resorting and packing gear, we hit the trailhead a few miles from Penitentes. Mules were waiting for us, eager to carry our gear on their backs so we could stroll leisurely over the 35 miles to base camp in scenery described as, "Spectacular glaciers contrasting with a desert backdrop make this approach both surreal and unforgettable." It was.

Our approach to the mountain was up a seldom-used trail along the Guanacos River. Most expeditions take the shorter route from the western side. Our longer scenic route provided time to assess why I chose to give up a thermo-controlled environment, oxygen and fast foods for what seemed, at times, like wandering 40 years in a wilderness. The three-day hike to base camp was in hot, dry, windy conditions under a burning sun, but as we gradually gained elevation, the temperature dropped accordingly.

You do get more bang for the buck taking the longer route. Upon arriving at the 12,500-foot base camp, your body has been banged up a bit, but in comparison, that part of the journey is no more demanding than a stroll through Central Park.

As elevation increases, your body begins objecting, and your head agrees, but it doesn't know enough to turn back. At base camp, we re-sorted the gear again in order to take only the essentials up the mountain. Like the camels at K2, mules can't go beyond base camp, at which time you become a lowly pack beast. The mules eventually returned our excess gear to the hotel to await our return from the summit. Therefore, it was necessary to assume the physical prowess of a pack mule. When you do this, your mental ability has regressed to a level nearly comparable to that of an un-schooled mule. Which one was dumber, me, or our mules back at the hotel eating a steak smothered in alfalfa?

Carrying 15-20 pounds in a daypack is easy. I made it to base camp in decent condition, but began to feel the effects of nearly 13,000 feet of elevation. Moving the body at that altitude required twice as much effort as at the level where God originally planned for man to live, hunt and gather.

To acclimatize and proceed on up, we followed the climb-high, sleep-low procedure. From base camp, we carried about half the gear to a higher camp, returned to our tents, ate, slept and then carried the tents and remaining gear to the next high camp. So we're going to spend this wonderful day carrying stuff up to the next camp, go back down, eat and sleep again and climb back up again the next day. It didn't make sense to leisurely carry 20 pounds to base camp, and then become an animal carrying 50 pounds from there.

My notes were brief. "Took gear up to 15,500 and back down. Did OK, but totally exhausted." The word "exhausted" was underlined. The first day from base camp took something from me. Is this what aging is all about? I want no part of it. However, I was up bright and early the next day, with full speed ahead for maybe the first half hour.

After arriving at Camp II, I recorded: "Thought about giving it up to prior exhaustion, weak. Struggled to lunch break. Laura reminded to use the rest-step (move one foot up a couple of feet and then the other up to the higher foot and then pause) and Amelio adjusted my pack. Worked wonders and a miracle. Tired but felt good and optimistic."

Although I knew the rest step, I'd quit using it. This step resembles walking up steps, but when you lift one leg to the next step, you bring the other leg to the same step and pause with both feet planted there for a couple seconds. It helps and is somewhat more restful than charging up like you are going for the gold at the Olympics and finishing on a stretcher. And if your pack is not balanced and set properly on your back, it seems to nearly double in weight.

Although Aconcagua is a walk-up or non-technical mountain, we wore our heavy plastic climbing boots and carried the spiked crampons to attach in case we encountered ice and snow. The climb was primarily over mazes, clumps of small and large rocks and scree, which is an accumulation of loose stones and rocky debris that is slippery as ice. Each step is placed selectively. To make matters worse, one of my climbing boots began rubbing the skin off one of my heels. You take every precaution in preparation—silk liner socks and outer wool socks—because when your feet go, you go with them. Oh well, what's skin off your heel, which is merely a flimsy covering for your bones.

As mentioned, the hotel in the mountains from which we departed was at a small village known as Penitentes, a name originating from a freak of nature. Charles Darwin observed and wrote about penitentes when he explored the area in 1839. A penitente is a tall thin blade of hardened snow and ice protruding up toward the sun like a pure white pinnacle. Atmospheric and changing climatic conditions form these spires, some taller than one's head. The landscape was arid, barren and dust colored, but these strange and sizeable fields of penitentes frequently blocked our way, which made it tougher to maneuver. It was like scrambling, pushing and shoving through a blockade of hungry, ghost-like icy tall daggers objecting to the intrusion.

What is wrong with me? I remember Pyramide Blanca, Huayna Potosi, Everest, K2 and the others. They were hills like the ones I ran over as a child on the farm. My grandfather trained me to herd sheep and cows like a dog, slobbering, barking and nipping at their heels. In my younger days, I was like a lion circling an antelope. What changed me to a pussycat?

Taking these kinds of trips requires clearance from a doctor. My doctor doesn't want to see me. As I write, I made an appointment to see him a couple of weeks ago. He's a 50-year-old kid I had in school and takes good care of me. I explained I was unhappy with my running. I was experiencing a loss of stamina, speed and shortness of breath. He told me to leave his office so he could treat sick people.

I've been a very fortunate and lucky guy, but Aconcagua was my Waterloo. I can empathize with Napoleon now that I've been exiled, too.

If it wasn't for the heavy pack and the climbing boots and my legs, arms and brain, I could have sprinted to the top. We'd left the second high camp early that morning with two more camps to go. Carrying only the essentials, three of us slept in a two-man tent, but I slept well and ate well at breakfast served picnic style, like when your family throws a blanket on the ground in a park, opens a basket and eats dainties under a tree cooled by a gentle, summer breeze. The breakfast on the mountain was a bowl of a grain product, and you either stood up to eat or sat on an outdoor rock as a cold wind turned your hot mush into slush. Better to spend your pension check there than at Wal-Mart.

Food on a 16-day climb for 14 people had to be well planned and nourishing. Breakfasts usually consisted of hot granola or oats, cookies and hot coffee or tea. Since we'd be climbing, we each carried our lunches, which were usually crackers, cookies and tins of cheese, salami, herring or pate' topped off with chocolate. Dinners consisted of hot soup, potatoes, and couscous or rice dishes served with sauces, spices and grated cheese with cans of mixed vegetables. Most any food tastes good after a day on a mountain.

At Camp II, my 45-pound pack gained at least 15 more pounds over night. On all my other trips, porters had carried the bulk of the gear and supplies. On Huayna Potosi, I had carried a heavy pack from 16,000 feet to 18,000 feet, and considered it one of the most physically demanding ordeals I'd ever encountered. I was seven years younger then and in my prime, which you reach at age 64. Two and a half years before, at K2, I carried a heavy pack from base camp to the advanced base camp and did quite well. The laws of physics designed by God and governed by the mathematical formula—aging plus added weight equals inertia—meant nothing to me. It was not that I didn't believe in God, or evolution or physics, but some of those laws don't apply to me, and never have.

It was not disease, starvation or war that killed me; it was the altitude, the steep unpaved road, the weather, the absence of the stupid mules, the lack of red meat and the hideous pack. After a few hours, we stopped for a break. Wes called me aside and asked if I thought I could make it. He said he'd been observing me weaving and struggling. I was. The decision was to send me down.

I was left alone huddled against the wind between two boulders, humiliated, weakened and a failure. I was a child in a little league game striking out, a student failing a physics test, a runner collapsing before breaking the tape, losing the gold. Would they leave me to die on the mountain? No, but I was greatly disappointed. Perhaps my competitive nature had taken me that far, no crying shame. Competing is to win or lose. Maybe wining is giving it all during the journey. I sat on the rocks in the loneliest place for about three hours with nothing to accompany me but my thoughts.

Wes designated Laura to accompany, assist and insure I got back to Penitentes, where my life would continue. The plan was that Laura would dump the gear out of her pack and go on up to the next camp, where we'd carried gear the day before. She'd fill her empty pack with the essentials for our survival and come back down to lonely me.

Laura was an extraordinary individual, and perhaps one of the strongest young ladies I've ever known. In her 24 years, she had had more outdoor experiences in the wild than perhaps 99.5 percent of the population would have in a lifetime. She was well trained in all outdoor activities and a graduate from Prescott University in Arizona. The school is noted for its outdoor and adventure-based education programs, including wilderness leadership. Upon enrolling, Laura began a three-week adventure into Arizona's wilderness as an introduction and orientation to surviving in a wilderness. She was as comfortable and confident in that setting as I would be in my cozy home with my wife periodically asking, "Can I get you anything?"

Desperately needing someone trained in wilderness leadership, I kept waiting and wondering if she would return. All sorts of thoughts raced through my mind. What if she was injured or lost? What if an angry god decided to sacrifice me? The Incas sacrificed people in those same mountains. I can see it now, "Old American warrior sacrificed in ancient heathen ritual near sacred mountain in South America," or "When found, delirious man jumped to his death before they could grab him."

We were located in the area near where a Uruguayan plane crashed in 1972. There are books and a movie about this flight disaster known as the Miracle in the Andes. Although planes searched for the missing craft, it wasn't detected, because the downed plane was painted white and had crashed into the snow. Only 16 of the 45 passengers survived. Before found, these 16 stayed alive for 72 days by living on those who had died.

Laura, my only hope and substitute savior, finally appeared, ambling down the mountain.

"We'd better get as far down as we can with what's remaining of the day," she said. She dumped the retrieved gear from the higher camp beside the gear she'd left behind and told me to dump the stuff in my pack alongside. The pile would have been a burden for a stubborn mule. We then repacked—stuffed—our two empty packs for the five-day trek back to Penitentes, and plumbing, heat, soap, plates and forks used for properly eating delicious foods at a wooden table instead of one made from a God-designed rock.

"Put it on," she said.

"Put what on?" I asked.

"The pack," she said.

I reached over and could barely lift it. On the second try, it nearly crushed me, but I wobbled and struggled, and with her help, swung it up over my back. You say it's five days? Tell my family I love them and not to waste time looking for me. Searchers discover dead bodies many years later when glaciers melt.

We're going down, not up, so if I lose my balance, I'll slide to the bottom. I've mentioned the difficulty, the wear and tear on the body, particularly on the legs. The more weight carried, the greater the pressure. Pay utmost attention, or else the echo of the splat is heard from the bottom three minutes later.

We carried a tent, two sleeping bags, thermal pads, all of our down clothing for the summit, boots other than the climbing boots we wore, food for five days, a stove, fuel, two bowls and two spoons, two cooking pots, personal items and I carried a New Testament.

If I were stuck on a mountain, without reading materials, the Lord might help me get down if he observed me open the New Testament. How could *War and Peace* help? It's too heavy. Every extra ounce carried up the mountains is eliminated, and that is one of the reasons I took a small Gideon's New Testament. It's heavy, too, when you read it. What did I learn? Many things, including in today's parlance, Paul and Luke were cool dudes.

What a day! Laura and I found a level spot to camp for the night. I dropped my backbreaking pack and collapsed. After I managed to help her put up our tent, I fell onto my sleeping bag inside the tent, too weary to remove my boots. Laura lit our little stove and cooked a pot of hot food, and I spooned it down, although it took all my remaining strength. What happened to me? Never had I failed to wolf down food when famished.

There we were, a 71-year-old codger, and a 24-year-old young lady crammed in a tent, an odd couple if ever there was one. There is an unwritten honor system in the wild. Males and females sleep in the same tent when the situation dictates. Bob and Steve slept in a tent with Hun Su, a beautiful lady from South Korea, who didn't speak English. Such is the adventurous presence of other real people. Privacy is privacy no matter where, and any violation is a cardinal sin. A climbing culture is like no other. Individual lives become intertwined quickly since your own welfare and life may be dependent on the others. It's always a brother-brother, brother-sister arrangement.

I awakened at the break of day, which was good and bad—good that I was alive and bad that we were four days from that little part of heaven located in Penitentes. Not only that, we'd have to fight our way through acres of penitentes, similar to Don Quixote fighting the windmills.

Although too tired to record much in my journal, I scribbled a few notes: "Weak, weak with 60 pounds, she has 70. Every step pressure and blister painful. Scree, loose rock and penitentes up to seven feet tall, tough to get through. Every step a struggle, many times don't know if I can go another. Must get to Camp I."

Sleep restores, but not completely. Then it was a new day. Laura cooked hot granola with powered milk, and we departed for Camp I, the next camp several miles above base camp and our goal. We planned to pick up extra food at the base camp that had been stored, and, thank God, leave some of our unneeded gear for the mules to take back.

I grew up with mules on the farm, but my grandfather decided to sell them and rely on horses to pull our wagons and plows. Mules can be cantankerous and stubborn. After all these years, I'm thankful they're so stupid. However, they are intelligent enough never to carry a load higher than a base camp.

The second day descending was uneventful other than slashing our way through those God-awful penitentes, the inverted ice daggers that will pierce your heart. Although my strength was beginning to return, my legs were battered to the point they seemed to beg for amputation. Down and down, but brace yourself, or be introduced to oblivion.

Is that the base camp down there? Glory to God in the highest! I knew the New Testament would pay off. The base camp appeared to be a half-mile away? Elevation affects your eyesight; a half-mile is two.

At last, the promised land! We dropped our packs on the ground, a feeling like when a prisoner is unchained from a prison cell. We were alongside the Vacas River as it raged from its origin up the mountains. The 35 miles to go would be much easier with our packs reduced from 60-70 pounds to about

30 each. The elevation would gradually decline from 12,500 feet at base camp down the valley with a drop of 5,000 feet and down hill all the way. Glory, hallelujah! Forty years in the wilderness and I'm Moses. No, he didn't make it to the land of promise. I'll be Joshua, who did.

After a good night's sleep, Laura and I repacked again. Every day, we sort gear, pack and repack, a ritual like showering, shaving and preparing for work. Extra food and other items had been stored in plastic barrels at base camp. We stored our climbing boots, crampons, ice axes and heavy clothing there for the mules to take back. We packed three days supply of food and only the essentials for the final three-day trek.

Oh, what a beautiful morning—everything's going my way, etc, etc. Our packs seemed as light as a load of balloons. With the heaviest stuff stored for the mules, the oxygen supply practically doubled and as a warm morning sun greeted us, Laura and I began our three-day stroll down the remote Vacas Valley.

Although it was a dry, desert-like setting, in places the main route was blocked by mudslides. The summer melting of glaciers and snow had created a few furrows and ridges of mud. Some were knee deep, which required going around them. We had gone no further than a half mile when we encountered a mudslide blocking our way. It was either a long trek up the mountain or down into the rapidly flowing Vacas River to wade along the bank in hip-deep water. Won't my shoes and clothes get wet? Yes, they will, but that's why we're blessed with the original drying mechanism known as the sun.

We entered the cold water, which seemed to be flowing at the speed of light, and began placing cautious steps around the rocks and boulders in the raging river. I am not normally an on-the-spot prayer person, but I asked God that if he would keep me upright, I'd do my best to remain in that position from that day forward.

After the sun had disappeared behind the mountains, Laura said, "We'll camp over there," pointing across the river. When we camped there on the way up, the mules took us across. Where's a mule when you need one?

"If you lose your balance when crossing this river, immediately release your pack, because it can drag you down to your death," she said. Laura knew most everything. I prayed twice that day. I didn't expect a miracle, but if God could part the Red Sea and Jesus walk on water, he could find a way for me. Using our hiking sticks as third legs, each challenging step was touch and feel amidst the underwater boulders. I was not totally immersed during this baptism, but temporarily cleansed of many sins.

Later in the afternoon, we set up camp, changed to dry clothes and placed our only pair of hiking boots out to dry—they didn't. I was still weak, but my legs were beginning to regain strength. Nonetheless, I collapsed on the sleeping bag while Laura lit the little stove, made dinner, and served a delicious hot soup, followed by red beans and rice with salsa and cheese. She was amazing. With two easier days to the village, I thought I could make it.

The next day was sunny and bright. We departed camp early, and later, when we stopped for a break, Laura pointed and quietly said, "Look over there." I didn't see anything unusual. She kept pointing without excessive movement. "See the guanacos?" It was standing about 100 yards away and camouflaged against the rocks on the side of a hill. It's a treat to see a guanacos, which is a cousin to the llama. They are distinct to that area, quite skittish and rarely observed. It was another "wow" moment, like the time Ang Porba spotted the blue sheep at Everest.

We made it to the trailhead and waited a couple of hours for the five-mile ride to the hotel and a shower. I didn't necessarily need a shower. If the Vacas River doesn't cleanse you, nothing will.

When Wes said, "I think you need to go back down," it was difficult to accept. A bruised and battered body meeting its limits compounds the damage to one's pride and ego. But it's not whether you win or lose, it's how you play the game. Whoever said that didn't know what he was talking about. Why keep score? Reach the summit and it's a peak victory; turning back is a humiliating defeat.

Victory is making the winning goal in the final second, the last step to the summit. Ten of our group of 14 reached the highest peak in the Western Hemisphere and celebrated victory. Three days later, we all met together for a joyous reunion back in Mendoza before departing to our homes. The final score was unimportant; the team was a resounding winner. Although banished to the locker room, like a star player with a sprained ankle, my teammates played on to the final gun. The guys on the bench joined the celebration of the team's victory.

My memories are winning ones. When Laura and I came down the mountain, we were all alone in the stunning setting, in the domain of pure nature's prominent splendor and solitude. We carried the life-sustaining necessities on our backs, and we carried that other vital quality described by Emerson, "The joy of your spirit is the indication of your strength." I was weak, but strong, because the joy of the spirit is the greatest gift.

When you are out hiking where the terrain is rugged and steep, as a safety precaution, remember, don't look up. You never know what you'll find looking down. As mentioned before, I have several objects and mementos on my desk, found in several places throughout the world that bring back the memories. On a shelf five feet away is, of all things, a mule shoe. Not only do I remember Jack and Jenny on our farm 65 years ago, every day when I see the mule shoe I found on the mountain near Aconcogua, it remains an enduring symbol of my luck and good fortune.

It brought me luck when Laura guided me down the mountain. Scanning through some of my scribbled notes, I discovered this thought and tribute to her, "You brought me safely down the mountain, but the essence of your humanity lifted me to the highest summit."

It was a marvelous journey, but all journeys and adventures end. Then you plan and prepare for the next one—whatever the age.

CHAPTER 12

IT WAS A GRAND DAY IN MY LIFE

❖ ❖ ❖

Accomplishing something makes us feel good. At age 76, you'll need all the help you can get to accomplish getting out of bed. Once you're out and your weight is equally distributed on both feet without swaying back and forth, you can take the next step, if you can remember where you wanted to go.

By this late age, you've learned there are 24 hours in a day. Say nine hours are at sleep, including the one-hour body shut down after lunch. You'll need hours to run errands and two to eat. Figuring in no more than three hours messing with your computer and dozing in front of the television, there are seven hours remaining in your day. Golda Meir said that being 70 is not a sin, but after that age, there are not that many sins you can commit, such as carousing or sexual promiscuity. If those seven extra hours are spent accomplishing something and achieving, the chance of having good days are significantly increased. There's so much out there you can do; volunteering, hobbies, reading, writing, travel and education. Take on a long-term project and pursue it with a passion, which is not a sin. If your passion gland is inactive, wake it up. Mine is uncontrollable.

After living 76 years—over 27,000 days and count-ing—I've certainly had more than my fair share of the good, great and grand days. Supposedly, a day is what we make it. If that is true, then retirement is like a marriage; we have to work at it. But who ever got married to work like crazy at something other than your job? I'd rather think retirement is like a poker game. If you know when to hold them and when to fold them and some other tricks, you can learn how to stack the deck and hit the jackpot.

Excluding politicians, it seems like everybody else wants us to have a good day. It's about the only thing a grocery bagger says to you. Have you noticed that fast-food personnel have upped it a bit? Not only have a good day, but while you're having it, make it a "wonderful" one. Although it's nobody's business, how many "have-a-good-day(s)" do you get each day? I respond, "You, too," and get on with my busy life. Or, when you're feeling lousy and go to the doctor, the first thing the trained receptionist asks, "How are you today?"

"Great, but I didn't have anything else to do so I thought I'd stop by and wish everyone in this office a good day."

On Fridays, the public wants us to, "Have a good weekend." What's the big deal about a weekend? Getting a good start on the first day of a week is what counts. How come Mondays are usually excluded from wishing strangers something good? And what does, "Have a good one," mean? One what, day, night, week, year or life? Let's simplify the whole charade and say, "Have a good life," and be done with it.

Having a good day is a day-to-day thing. If you live 34,675 days to age 96, over 34,000 should have been good ones. I have three friends in their mid-90's. They are healthy, sharp and active. They seem to have skipped dementia and continue living the good life. No way to accomplish that if there were very many "It-was-one-of-those days" thrown in.

One difference between now and back then is that when you ask a grandkid what kind of day he's having, it's limited to one of two types—fun or boring. In this modern age, boring ones outnumber their fun days nine to one. When I was growing up on the farm, six days per week were workdays as God commanded, and the seventh was church in the morning, barn-lot baseball in the afternoon and church again that evening. We needed two fiery sermons each Sabbath day to restrict sinfulness during the next six. This plan worked well, because God was keeping your score.

During the week, our animals, crops, gardens, woods, creeks and nature's wonders were never boring. Fun time was anticipating and going to town on Saturday night. A bag of popcorn at the Western shoot-em-up movie followed by a double-dip ice cream cone topped off a great week.

Does a horse have a bad day, or your dog? We don't know, but we do know our complex nervous system is designed to react and respond to the gamut of all kinds of days, including those that are so-so, same-old, one of those, you wouldn't believe it, bad, dismal, a drag, the pits, disastrous and tragic. If most of your days are OK, that's OK, but during retirement, you'll need to avoid routine and boredom. I prefer the good days, occasional great ones and a grand day now and then. Max Buxbaum explained, "Some people, no matter how old they get, never lose their beauty—they merely move it from their faces to their hearts." The beauty of retirement is like the line in the song; "It can come true and can happen to you if you're young at heart." It's true.

As the years pass by, memories of the good times remain. After retiring, our previous 13,109 days on the job soon fade into a blurry haze. Successful retirement requires considerable planning and effort to insure the next 11,680 (after age 95, fatigue might get you) days never dip below good or OK. Keep score, and if "one-of-those-days" or worse is filling up your chart, then you should undergo self-analysis or consider becoming active in Aging Anonymous. It's not counting the days, but making the remaining ones count.

After age 76, we spend more time in a recliner with special padding contoured for the relief of arthritic pain. Use some of those quiet moments to think about your life. Do the good and grand days stand out? Mine do. My birth was a grand day and all subsequent birthdays were special ones. At some point, usually in the 40's, we tend to begin ignoring birthdays, because the 50th is usually considered the over-the-hill day. On that day, we begin assessing facts and figures in anticipation of our second life. The fact is, as we approach 60, work often becomes tiring and a drag. We then begin to look at the figures on our balance sheet. If they add up, we contact the pension offices and set a date.

Looking back on my past life—looking ahead doesn't twist your neck—it seems as if I didn't plan much of anything. Life happened and I took it as it came. It was as if my wife and four children suddenly popped out from behind a curtain, and there they were. What do I do with them? Life was moving so fast back then, I never had the time to sit down at a drawing board. The boss and the bosses at home had my day planned out. Then retirement day, and I'm on my own. It's a whole new experience and responsibility. You mean I get to choose what kind of day I'll have? Yes, you do. Think it through.

My life was and is good. Recalling the early years, perhaps one of the best moments was when I was very close to maturity and inserted my first driver's license in my billfold. It was a more exciting day than when I signed my marriage license. My driver's license was so important to me that I placed it beside Rosie's picture.

You can fall in love on a lonely country road parked under a full moon, which leaves you so full of feelings you need to let them out. However, when Rosie drops you for another, it's like you're an older person who has fallen and can't get up. If it's true that maddening love results in disaster, what hope is there?

The first day of first grade, high school and college are unforgettable. In 1952, a country boy from a small high school in the hills of Kentucky walked onto a campus where the hallowed halls of ivy and the classes he was enrolled in loomed high over his head. I did not want to appear as a misfit or a country hick so I wore a sports coat and a white stiff-collared shirt with a clip-on bow tie. I soon noticed the other Joe College guys strolling through the campus were not wearing chokers, so I jerked off my bow tie and discreetly tucked it in my pocket. My first higher-education lesson was a valuable one; go with the flow.

I don't remember who asked whom, but I remember standing at an altar watching a blond-haired beauty dressed in a hand-me down wedding gown ambling provocatively toward me. Yes, I'd obey her and everything, but please get on with it. Guests wished us many long years of happiness, prosperity, bliss, etc., but happiness in the moment is what counts. Happiness is also two people combined into one flesh, isn't it? Joined together on paper, we rushed to a car wash to get the shoe polish washed off our borrowed honeymoon car. When the blissful married couple got out of the car, two other nearby moving cars crashed. Could this be symbolic of something now, or later? It's been 56 years of leaky radiators, dead batteries and fender benders, but no head-on collisions yet.

When the U.S. Navy needed me to help protect my wife and country, I went. My bride waited longingly for my safe return, at which time I was way behind with my future, and not caught up yet. The day I was honorably discharged from the Navy was a grand day. I had not seen my nine-month-old daughter for five months. My family met me at the airport. On the ride home, my daughter sat on my lap, staring quietly and inquisitively as if asking, "Who is this strange guy?"

"I'm your daddy." Being a daddy requires you sign a wavier granting all your rights and freedoms to your wife and children, who then have the power of attorney.

Eighteen years later, I took my only daughter to a large university and moved her into a coed dorm. I had to kick beer cans out of the hallway to prevent tripping. I told her to remember everything I had taught her about temptation, dumped her off and drove home in prayer again. Had I lived in a coed dormitory this book would be titled, *Dorms are a Blast – If You Don't Burn Out.* Four years later, my daughter began teaching English on the Navajo reservation in New Mexico. Daddies worry about their little girls wherever they are, especially when they're out of sight.

My first-born son went to the same university my daughter attended and became a quantitative analysis specialist. I have no idea what he does. I'm a qualitative person, and an expert at analyzing the quality of retired life. What's quantity of life without quality?

My twin sons were born on a cold, snowy December night. Our country doctor was competent, but noted for being a man of few words. After an examination about all he would say was, "Take these pills." When he came to the waiting room to announce the healthy arrival of my two new sons, he was unusually expressive and elated. It had been a "four-for-one" day for him. That morning, he ran across the street to the office of another small-town doctor, who had been called out of his office. Our doctor delivered twin girls in the other doctor's office. Delivering two sets of twins in one day is a great one.

All four of my smart children passed the driver's test, and all four wrecked at least one of my cars soon thereafter. I'll skip the chapter on police reports, outrageous insurance premiums and body shop estimates. Smashed cars containing human bodies inside without a scratch are grand days any day.

There are over 10,000 high-school graduates I helped coax, push and force out into this wonderfully crazy world of ours. Not one lacked potential. Getting that across was half the battle. There are good days and bad days wherever you are, but at least 300 of the over 6,000 days I spent in high schools were like what used to happen in the Roman Coliseum. Forget the day they turned the pig loose in the school, and the day someone poured vodka in the orange juice at an early morning senior-class officer's meeting.

To effectively relate to the high school age group, you need to revert to their maturity level since they are years away from attaining yours. Convincing the young they have a promising future resulting in a good life is the other half of the battle. Maintaining a sense of humor in stressful times helps lighten the load, which sets a foundation for the good days ahead.

Throughout our lives, we experience those days unlike any others. They are the different, unique, strange, exciting or thrilling ones we can't forget. Erase those not worth remembering like you do with the delete button on your computer. Remember the grand day you fired up your first computer? Remember the frustration? Forget it.

Gifts make a difference any day. I piled my four kids in the back seat of my old used Pontiac Catalina and hurried to Florida to relax. After being half relaxed, we headed back home. Somewhere in Georgia, my Catalina began to sputter. I pulled into a ramshackle filling station, and a good old boy saw the steam pouring out and looked under the hood. He told me he could fix it between the times he didn't have to pump gas. My family went to a shade tree and ate Georgia peaches for about an hour. The good old boy replaced a gasket and told me I could hit the road, that my Catalina, with its few rust spots, was like new.

"Thanks, and how much do I owe you?"

With grease dripping down his arms, he thought for a moment and said, "Oh, nothing. You've had enough bad luck for one day." Good old boys know how to teach valuable lessons.

Possibly the finest gift I ever received came during those most difficult days when family members were across the seas fighting in World War II. In addition to making many material sacrifices, a constant concern was the anxiety caused by knowing that not all of our fathers, uncles and cousins would return. Two of my cousins gave their lives. During those darkest hours of the war, when I was about nine or ten, I'd hurry to the mailbox each day hoping we'd received a letter from Uncle John in Germany or from another of our several kin far away. There had never been a package addressed to me before, but there it was. How did my Uncle Jim know I dreamed about a baseball glove? I've never received a gift, a treasure, that meant more to me than the new glove and ball from him.

It's a good day when you live to see another. My wife is a water person; I prefer the land and the higher the better. I'd rather climb than sink. I agreed to accompany her on a deep-sea diving expedition in the Gulf of Mexico. She would dive, and, although I'd never done it before, I would snorkel above the divers in blue water, which they say is like relaxing on a cloud as it drifts through a blue sky. The first day went great as two others and I snorkeled over the divers watching them do their thing on the bottom. Clear water and fish are nearly as beautiful as a mountain covered in snow.

When the boat dumped us into the water the second day, the waves began churning like the cream did when we used to make butter. The three of us who were on top of the water began drifting away from the boat as the waves and swells thrashed and rolled causing the divers and boat to disappear. I began to look for land and spotted it two or three miles away. The first survival rule is; don't panic. I didn't, because we'd hear the motors of the search planes any minute, wouldn't we? A small boat out of nowhere picked us up, and eventually located our boat.

"We knew where you were all the time," the boat guy said firmly. Yeah, we were in the Gulf of Mexico. If God had intended us to be amphibious, in addition to arms and legs, we would have evolved with fins and a flipper.

Siberia may be at the bottom of your travel list, but it was near the top of mine. After five days and nights on the Trans-Siberian Express, our group of educators reached our destination in Khabarovsk near the eastern edge of the Soviet Union. After checking into a hotel, we went to dinner. Two cooks brought out one of the largest birthday cakes I'd ever seen. The cake, covered with thick white icing, was inscribed in brilliant yellow with, "Happy Birthday Terry." How did they know it was my birthday unless our guide on the train phoned ahead? And why did they take considerable time and effort to surprise and please me? Weren't we in a Cold War with the communists? No, "we" weren't, but the Kremlin and the White House were.

Siberia is huge, and the flight back to Moscow spanned 11 time zones. I dreaded the long flight crammed in a small seat on a crowded Aeroflot. Soon after we were up and over the tundra, the hostess began passing out tall glasses and asking, "Juice or vodka?" Then she'd pour the glasses nearly three/fourths full of our preference. On long flights, juice makes me nauseous. After consuming a couple glasses of clear liquid fire, I rode a rocket ship back to Moscow. It was a very good day.

I'll never forget the time I saw her electrifying smile from across the crowded room during that enchanting afternoon. My wife was spending a year in England as a Fulbright exchange teacher while I kept the home fires burning and a garden growing. She called and asked if I wanted to fly over and escort her to a garden party. I can grow the best tomatoes and corn you've ever tasted, but I'd never partied in a garden before.

Vera read the invitation: "To have the honour to meet Her Royal Highness, The Princess of Wales, Her Majesty's Government in the United Kingdom of Great Britain and Northern Ireland request the pleasure of the company of Mr. and Mrs. Cummins at a Garden Party at Lancaster House, St James L W1 on Friday 28 June at 2:30. Informal Day Dress."

"Is the Princess of Wales, who I think she is?" I asked.

"Yes, it's Diana."

"What's informal day dress?"

I'm not a wild party guy, but why not? I grabbed a plane.

My wife and I spruced up in informal day dress as best we could and took the train from Guilford, where she taught, to London. Security had roped off the entrance to the Lancaster House as throngs of people waited to get a glimpse of the Princess. I flashed my pass and walked through the mob as if I were important, like a consulate or an ambassadorial official negotiating a trade or peace agreement

"Don't embarrass me," warned my wife.

She knows I'm quiet, shy and reserved, but possess latent country-bumpkin behaviors stemming from my roots. When they surface, it's often at inopportune times.

The guidelines from the Royal Office explained the Princess would personally meet each of the Fulbright exchange teachers while spouses were to remain on the periphery. When I party, it's never on the periphery. Why go?

Elegant tables covered with linens, dainty finger foods and tea had been prepared. I was hungry from the start, but the instructions explained not to eat until the Princess went first. I didn't think she'd ever go. It took about two hours for her to meet each teacher, asking silly questions and getting sillier answers.

Although I remained on the periphery, I was leery of doing or saying something stupid, so I stood around staring at the people in their informal day finery. When this got old, I decided to break out of my thick, protective shell and mix it up. When I'm in a stiff social setting, it's difficult for me to perform in an etiquette mode, but what the heck. I began wandering around as if I owned the place, asking questions like what time is it, or when do you think we'll get to eat?

One affable gentleman had several medals hanging from his coat. I went over to him and asked, "How's it going?" He knew immediately I was from a foreign country. There can be communication problems when one speaks a Kentucky dialect and the other pure English. If he said, "It's a bloody good day," I think it means the day was very good. If I said, "The day was bloody," it means the day was bloody. We hit it off and had a jolly good time chatting and joshing. I explained that when Sir Walter Raleigh introduced tobacco to England, he imported it from our farm. I also told him I'd observed him making a concerted effort to charm all the beautiful ladies in attendance. He said the same about me.

After our conversation, I asked someone, "Who was that guy?"

"Didn't you know? He's the Lord Mayor of London."

If the Lord Mayor and I hit it off, why not try the Princess? Hoping she would acknowledge or speak to me, I maneuvered over to stand near her. She was nearly as tall as I am, and as I approached Her Majesty, she turned toward me. It was so exciting when, for one split second, I think we made eye contact. That's as close to royalty as I've ever been, although I did get within 20 feet of John F. Kennedy and within 100 feet of Bill Clinton when he was on the prowl.

❖ ❖ ❖

Upon retirement, my good, great and grand days began piling up despite the woes of aging, which require a calendar full of office visits. We need to draw your blood. You drew it yesterday. We need some more. If it's not a hearing aid or cataracts, it's a root canal, knee replacement or a leaky valve. And your blood may begin to clot. To prevent a clot from settling in your brain, thin your blood. When you have your blood thinned, you may also need to thicken your muscles and bones to prevent breaking something. If you have weight, don't eat. And you might notice that your pacing is not what it was, which may require having a pacemaker inserted in your chest. After they cut and paste different parts of your body, it might look something like a Picasso. But your heart is the key. Its health depends upon a rhythmic attitudinal beat, which keeps its beauty alive.

If you can, avoid the time-consuming admission process to overnight stays in a Hospitable Hospital Inn. One last time—diet and exercise is about all you can do. Try to maintain your body on a permanent outpatient basis. Despite a calendar filled with appointments to check, repair or remove something, it's better than what's remaining of you being permanently removed. My day is coming, but lucky me, I've never spent a night in a gown opened at the back.

A retiree wakes up each morning to a new day. You don't have to go to the grocery to be wished a good day—wish it to yourself. Then get up and get with it. It doesn't matter what you accomplish, but it should be something that makes you feel good. Another trip to the mall followed by another episode of crashing on the couch and watching the news—Asia threatens Europe or the North Pole is getting mushy or Disney Land is under water—is not an accomplishment.

A regret I have is not volunteering for more worthy causes. As an active and long-time member of Rotary International, our club is always involved in various worldwide humanitarian projects and worthy ones in our own community. It is a structured way to give back something to those in need. For a time, I volunteered in assisting recording books for the blind and donated platelets to leukemia patients. All you have to do is lie down so they can stab each arm with a long needle. All your blood is then pumped out of your body and re-circulated through a machine where your platelets are spun out and collected. A healthy body begins replacing platelets immediately. It's a simple procedure if you can refrain from moving your arms for two hours. What if a fly lands on your nose? Unless you have a very long tongue, purse your mouth and try blowing air up toward your nose to knock it off.

Retirement is the time to do what you want to do. Perhaps I'm selfish, but I want to keep doing what I want to do. If what I do offers a bit of cheer, amusement and encouragement, then what I do is not all in vain.

We all have those good days and moments achieved by individual accomplishment—finishing a race, baking a birthday cake or tending a beautiful garden. Good Samaritan deeds are also good for what ails us. The simple is not complex. You're in a hurry as usual and see a car with the hood up. Let the next guy be the Good Samaritan; I did my good deed yesterday. If I stop, I'll be off schedule. OK, hit the brakes. When his car starts up, you put your jumper cables back in the trunk and move on down the road. The stranger's expression and appreciation makes you forget the disruption of your busy schedule

The consequence of a grand day is the integration of a particular time, moment or experience into a part of your soul. It's a high obliterating the lows. It's more than pleasure, delight and satisfaction. It's like a revelation with a touch of ecstasy, a wonder drug that never wears off.

On my summit days, my body descended, but my sprit abides on the peaks. My marriage day would not have been that special without the bride. Since that day, I've had thoughts of descending, but haven't. I'm still up there washing stuff off my car and painting walls whether they need it or not. Marriage is a no-retirement zone. On my release-from-work retirement day, I strained a ligament jumping up and down. I've also strained things jumping up and down with and at my children. Raising them were very good days, dependent upon their having very good days.

Most all adventures, journeys and experiences leave an impression, lasting or fleeting, favorable or otherwise. Those days that try one's soul should be pushed to a back burner, turned off and let cool. It seems the grand ones are filed away in our consciousness in a rather haphazard way. When recalled, one incident or moment, one embedded image, seemingly insignificant, is the one that will not go away.

My memorable days and experiences, particularly during my travels, culminated with the presence and response of other persons. Although living in vastly different cultures and speaking different languages, most all the people with whom I had contact and association were humble, kind, friendly, helpful and compassionate. It only takes one brief moment and connection with another to turn a day into an exceptional and satisfying one. The setting may be spectacular and the view stupendous, but the fusion or union with an accompanying person intensifies the experience. It's like the other person opens an entrance to a part of their soul and invites you in.

The apprehension, preparation and agony of running my first marathon are not what I remember. After crossing the finish line, the Marine Corp officer placed a medal around my neck, shook my hand and said, "Congratulations, sir." That said it all. I hear him in my dreams.

We have those moments like no other, the magic and precious ones. You enter your children's room and all is calm. The door opens to joy, bliss and peace, all in one. The impression and feeling is a convincing and secure one, with your children asleep, protected by the angels nearby.

There are uncommonly remarkable moments stamped indelibly in our consciousness. I cannot forget his eyes. Three weeks after my retirement day was the day when Pertemba and I reached the top of Kala Patar in Nepal. He was an elderly and gentle Sherpa, who usually hummed a Buddhist mantra along the way during our two-week trek to Mt. Everest. Our group left camp at an early hour that day and hiked the several miles over the long Khumbu glacier to above the Everest base camp, which was near the base of a smaller mountain called Kala Patar. Our goal was to reach the top of Kala Patar, considered the best view of Mt. Everest from the south. Pertemba and I went ahead of our group, and after an exhausting 2,000-foot climb, we reached the top of the 18,200-foot peak.

The view was magnificent and over-powering and more than I'd expected. While savoring the moment and catching our breath, I opened a pack of candy treats and offered some to Pertemba. As I poured pieces into his hand, some dropped to the ground. Quickly retrieving them, he rose and looked into my eyes. I'd flown half way around the world, trekked for weeks and climbed to the peak of Kala Patar to see the highest point on earth.

However, when he looked into my eyes, the expression of compassion and gratitude from this simple, humble Sherpa exceeded the intense and potent power flowing from the peak of Everest. When I reflect back on that grand day, I perceive a man permanently linked to me.

There are those places where nature's superior designs are displayed, revealing the magnificence of the grand scheme. Although unspoken, there is that uniting aspect of humanity, which is based on gestures, expressions and representation. The clarity of the message is unmistakable. Pertemba in Nepal and a photographer in India didn't speak my language, nor I theirs. However, an act of kindness speaks in a loud and clear voice.

Our month-long Rotary Group Study Exchange tour to India was near its end. At Moga in the Punjab, we'd completed three days of visits to schools, businesses and shrines and to overflowing tables several times each day and then parties late into each night. During our visit, a photographer followed me around as if we were leashed together. He was somewhat a nuisance clinging to me, but he began to grow on me in a positive way. Always with a warm smile, the photographer would motion to me to move here or there for a photo with various groups of people anxious to have their picture taken with a mythical "leader" from the mythical United States. What was I to do, pretend I was an important "somebody"? Well, the photographer was and we all are. I faked the leadership thing as many others do. My brief exposure to fame was more than I had bargained for. The limelight is blinding.

Satish, our driver, barreled out of Moga headed to the next town. After several miles, he swerved over to the side of the road. As he skidded to a stop, I thought perhaps he was avoiding another sacred cow bolting from the brush. While I was wondering why Satish had stopped, a motorcycle pulled up beside our van with the photographer sitting on the back. His considerate and thoughtful act took me by surprise, but said it all.

Legend has it that the Buddha agreed to meet with his many followers to explain the meaning of life. Later known as "The Flower Sermon," the Buddha walked out before the large gathering with a beautiful flower in his hand. He held the flower up for all to see. After pausing a moment, he walked away.

The photographer handed me a bouquet of flowers through the opened window. The moment was very brief, but long enough for me to see the humility and dignity of a man whose name I didn't know. The motorcycle revved up and sped away. When I recall the kindness, generosity and unalterable respect of the people in India, the image will not leave. The man made a journey to give flowers to me, and then like the Buddha, he went away.

The day after our arrival at the north face base camp at Mt. Everest in Tibet, our group had the option of taking a short, medium or long hike. Guess which group I joined? Libby, Bob and I departed camp early that morning guided by Ang Porba, our lead Sherpa.

Ang Porba was a strong, reserved and personable young Nepali who spoke English quite well. In 1979, at age 21, he was the youngest person to successfully summit Mt. Everest, and made three other unsuccessful attempts. He smiled when he told me that after his last attempt, "My wife made me quit climbing. She wants a live husband."

When hiking in the high mountains, many small rapidly flowing streams have to be crossed. The narrower ones can be jumped over, and with my long legs, I can jump across a six-foot stream. But slip on the slick rocks and you take a much-needed bath. Ang Porba, Libby and Bob had much shorter legs, so we had to throw large rocks in the wider streams for a makeshift bridge and then hope we stayed dry after our boots made contact with slanting, slick rocks. After the second of these wide streams, Libby and Bob decided they'd had enough excitement for one day, and hiked back to camp.

Ang Porba and I continued on in silence in the incredible setting. It was eerie and yet calm, peaceful and inviting, with an old guy struggling to follow a young Sherpa who was on familiar ground. He'd told me he wanted to explore other routes to Camp 1 and asked if I wanted to go. He had no need for me to tag along. I didn't want to be a burden, but my emotions were charged and my adrenaline flowing. My total focus and energies that grand day were directed toward following in his footsteps, but there were several times I questioned whether I had the stamina to continue. I did but more importantly, I had the will.

I was a little boy hurrying to keep up with Dad. It was like a line from one of Harry Chapin's songs, "We're going to have a good time now, Dad. We're going to have a good time now." To have that good time, I had to follow his lead. Nothing would please me more. Ang Porba took care of me that day, watched out for me and protected me, but I wanted more. I wanted to be worthy, not a burden. I wanted words of encouragement and approval. At rest stops, I'd attempt making conversation. Never appearing disinterested or discourteous, he would respond with few words, but seldom offered more than brief answers or comments. It was primarily a day of solitude. Perhaps a day wandering in the shadows of the Mother Goddess of the Earth is a time to absorb each powerful moment, take it all in. What is there to say? "Awesome" loses its effect after expressed the second time.

Ang Porba and I continued our exploration, he on a familiar and casual stroll and I on an unbelievable adventure in a fantasyland. It was like a Christmas morning with too many gifts to open. There were gifts for him, too. He suddenly stopped and shouted, "Wow, wow, wow!" Pointing across a steep ravine, again, "Wow, wow!" A flock of 17 rare bharal, also known as blue sheep, were scampering around and playing up on a high cliff. It was a "wow" scene, one of many that memorable day, which I later recorded as being, "a grand day in my life."

The next day, I recorded: "Many times I thought to myself, 'Darn you, I won't let you get away from me.' Then I could feel a power, a surge of energy from a source unknown. Ang Porba and I and Everest and the Rongbuk glacier and the seracs and the snow-capped peaks and the urge, the compelling call to climb, to soar, to be one with the power. As we continued on, he would pause and ask if I wanted to go higher,' and I'd reply, 'I m with you.'"

I'd lost all track of time. We had climbed to 19,000 feet or more, higher than Camp I. I stayed with him that long day, fording small streams and climbing and scrambling up one steep slope after another. My concentration and focus had been on following him. To avoid finding our way in darkness, he said that we'd better head back. Losing no time, he walked briskly down the glacier toward camp. Although my energy and adrenaline level had fallen to near empty, I followed. My body and legs were numb and listless, but my heart, mind and spirit remained in the highest place.

They seemed as stars twinkling in the night, the faint lights glowing softly from the lighted lanterns at our camp. Totally exhausted, but filled with emotion and elation, I had hoped Ang Porba might respond with something like, "You did well and I enjoyed being with you," but he quietly entered his tent without comment.

Our group had been resting at camp after their moderate morning hike and were assembled in the dining tent for dinner.

"Where have you been? We were worried about you."

"What a day," I replied, but there was no way I could adequately explain the kind of day it had been.

That night, I slept soundly and awakened early the next morning to a whisking sound. Susan, our group leader, and the Sherpas were brushing a fresh six-inch snowfall off our snow-covered tents.

Peering out from my tent—oh, what a sight! Often veiled in clouds, Everest stood naked, exposed, mighty and relentless. When the rich yellow-orange sun bathed its peak, it was like a uniting force signaling a closure to the old and an opening to a new, an invitation to a bright luminous presence. In that dramatic setting, my thoughts returned to yesterday when Ang Porba's presence illuminated another part of me.

We departed for Kathmandu and our journey's end. Two days later we stopped at Zangmu, a quaint mountain village on the Nepal-Tibet border, and checked into a one- half-star hotel. When we occasionally stayed in a hotel, the Shepas slept in tents. I had waited for an opportunity to give Ang Porba a gift of some sort at an appropriate time. Not carrying gifts, I decided to give him my watch. It was not an expensive one, but had some sentimental value. I used it for a stopwatch when I ran, and delighted in its display when it recorded a "fast" time for me.

Seeing Ang Porba unloading gear off to the side, I walked over, removed my watch and gave it to him: "I want you to have this for helping me."

Without any expression of emotion, he took the watch and said, "Thanks, uh, I guess I should put it on." That was it. Should I have expected, "You shouldn't have," or "Thanks so much," or "I don't know what to say?" With the watch in his hand, I hesitantly walked away, remembering a gift asks nothing in return.

Amidst all the bustle of unloading and sorting the bags and gear upon our arrival at the Shangri La Hotel in Kathmandu, I hung around the lobby waiting for Ang Porba to appear. The long-awaited hot shower, fresh clean clothes and dinner in a nice restaurant rather than in a cozy tent could wait. I had something more important to do; I had to say goodbye to Ang Porba, and, one last time, try to break through the barrier which shields a longing to fulfill a basic human need, acceptance and approval.

When I stepped out of the lobby for a brief moment and then returned, the Sherpas and Ang Porba were gone. It bothered me.

After a couple of days unwinding from our arduous trip, I went to the lobby to meet our group one last time for the last official function, the farewell dinner. All the Sherpas had scattered back to their homes, or so I'd thought. What a surprise! Appearing very pleased to see me, Ang Porba jumped up and rushed to me. Extending his hand, a gesture of recognition and confirmation, was sufficient in itself. What was there to say? Formed and shaped by an unassuming dignity of the highest sort, this humble man of few words conveyed and affirmed his guiding principle, the Buddhist attention and commitment to having respect and compassion, a concept genuinely expressed in conduct and deeds.

His gentle smile and the glow from his deep, dark eyes were like that clear, crisp morning a few days earlier when the sun came up, setting the peak of Everest ablaze, a clear focused beam, lighting another new day.

And then I saw it. Wow! He was wearing my watch, which was now his. Let's make it ours. It tracked the time that day, that grand day when Ang Porba took me to the mountain.

When the grand days on this earth end, what an adventure the next one will be!

POSTSCRIPT

❖ ❖ ❖

Remember earlier in this book when I bragged about never wearing a gown which opened at the back? Cancel it. About a month after finishing this book, something happened. My running had slowed to a plow-horse pace in the Derby race. The doctors checked me out and sent me to a place where I wore a gown open in the back that revealed not only my backside; it often crawled upward, which exposed things, for the most part, I've always tried to conceal. I don't want to talk about it.

Soon after the ordeal, I published an article exposing healthcare, which the government wants to control. The title: "A Nurse Named Awesome."

"Having lived over 76 years and never wearing a nightgown that opened at the back, I knew my day would come and it did. When the doctor looked under my hood, he said my heart was leaking and I needed a new valve job. When I asked how severe, he said it was similar to a major oil spill.

As a public service, I feel compelled to offer advice from the bottom of my torn heart so you will be equipped with an instructional guide if they ever open yours. First, you must go through the admission process to clarify your numerous privacy rights, which is a huge waste of time. After admission, they take you to a prep room and tell you to strip and put on a hospital gown. Undoubtedly, a committee of nudists under a narcotic influence designed these things. And remember this, hospitals are not in the restaurant business, they are in the healing business. If you go there to pig out, you will gain weight. The way they control this is by preparing food a pig would not eat. I lost ten pounds in ten days. (If blood, pain and suffering disturb you, skip to last paragraph.)

The reason skilled surgeons open your chest and heart, and maybe lay it out on a table for all I know, is to determine if and when closure is feasible for you. They repair leaking hearts with mechanical valves, or they use one from a pig or cow. I requested that if the surgeon inserted an animal part inside me, it be a mule valve, since mules were the toughest animal on our farm.

After completing the valve job, they use a set of jumper cables to shock your heart back into beating. If it does, is the mission accomplished? Maybe, but remember what happened in Iraq. Your body will look different, because numerous tubes will be sticking out of you like needles on a cactus. When you have to go to the bathroom, nurses carry your tubes and fluid containers in there with you. At this point, you have lost all rights except to remain silent. How can you remain silent with a couple of your tubes floating in the commode?

The operating room is the best part, because you never see it. The room after that is where you need to be knocked out again. My operation went well but then my oxygen level dropped and fluid began gathering around my lungs, so back to intensive care, where the intensity becomes overwhelming. Once when two doctors came in, one told me to get on the table and lie on my stomach so he could remove the fluid from my lungs. He held a large syringe with a five-inch needle.

'Now if I can stick this thing between his ribs… boom.' The nurse rushed over and told me to squeeze her hands Boom, boom and then he hit a rib and then another. As the nurse tried to get feeling back into her hands, I opened my eyes and saw a liter bottle over half full of fluid. One should keep a sense of humor no matter the circumstance. I asked, 'Is that Cherry Coke or Dr. Pepper?' What hurt the most was, no one laughed.

The second doctor took over and told me to turn over, explaining that he was going to insert a tube down to my right lung. He used a slit and slide process. I felt the tube slithering down, glancing and bumping into some of my other organs. It is conceivable that both these doctors had received terrorist training in Afghanistan before going on to med school.

My surgeon was like a god and my nurses were angels. When a new nurse bounced into my room, I asked her name. "Honey, you can just call me Awesome." She varied her greetings using either honey, sweetheart, or baby. I preferred "Baby" since I was so helpless. Awesome wore bright, flowery clothing, had that sultry wet-hair look and her eyes were sky blue with a tint of emerald green, which caused me to want to go out and romp with her amongst bees and birds on flowerbeds.

Awesome had depth, too. Her philosophy of life, "Don't sweat the small stuff."

"Do you think my stay here is small stuff?" I asked.

"You better believe it, Baby. When I nurse you back to health, I'll buy the first drink." Awesome was the best dose of medicine ever injected into my veins."

Twenty-seven days after the operation, my cardiologist checked me out at Veteran's Hospital. Her name was Jamie, and she was young, cute and chic. When I first met her, I thought she was a nurse until she said, "I'm your cardiologist, and how old are you?"

"I'm 76," I said.

"You don't look a day over 60," she said.

"And you don't look a day over 30," I said.

We were off to a great star, and it ended that way. Sixteen days after dismissal from the hospital, I asked, "When can I run again?"

"Today," she said.

It was a grand day in my life, and today is, too.

ACKNOWLEDGEMENTS

❖ ❖ ❖

Thanks to the Power, who provided the health and good fortune to light one fuse and then another. The gift of strong legs, lungs and heart were essential, and at times a lame brain helped, too. Although there may be other inhabitable planets, thanks to this World, to which I can testify, there could not be another as magnificent.

Thanks to Randy Smith, bookseller and publisher, who encouraged and inspired me to write this book. Thanks to the readers of the manuscript, Anne Caudill, Kathy Eichman, Bettye Weber and my daughter, Dani Cummins. They offered suggestions and encouragement and adjusted my comma faults. Readers keep an author humble when noting, "This makes no sense at all."

Thanks to my editors, Glenda Mills and Barbara O'Hara, who masterfully assisted me in organizing broken pieces into a structured whole.

One of my sons, Paul Curtis Cummins works as a graphic artist in California. I called him one day and asked if he would design the book cover, and explained what I had in mind. A few days later, he e-mailed the cover back. Thanks Curt!

OTHER BOOKS BY TERRY CUMMINS
Feed My Sheep
How Did Back Then Become Right Now?
Briny's Gift
Anne's Story is near completion.

Advanced Base Camp at K2, the
second highest mountain in the world

Base Camp at Mt. Everest near Rongbuk Monastery in Tibet

On the 19,000-foot Cayambe Summit in Ecuador

Climbing to the 20,000 summit of Huayna Potosi in Bolivia

Huayna Potosi summit bliss

Addressing students in India

Marine Corp Marathon, a finisher finished

After the Paris Marathon

Beginning a five-day journey back to civilization from Aconcagua, the highest mountain in the Western Hemisphere in Argentina

*Dad, Curt, Clint and Dani after
backpacking through the Grand Canyon*

8853337R0

Made in the USA
Charleston, SC
20 July 2011